Canadian Pilot's
Fitness Manual

Canadian Pilot's Fitness Manual

DAVID STEEN

Delacorte Press/Eleanor Friede

Published by
Delacorte Press/Eleanor Friede
1 Dag Hammarskjold Plaza
New York, N.Y. 10017

Manufactured in Canada

First printing

Library of Congress Cataloging in Publication Data

Steen, David.
  Canadian pilot's fitness manual.

  1. Air pilots — Diseases and hygiene. 2. Physical
fitness. 3. Exercise. 4. Air pilots — Medical
examinations — Canada. I. Canadian Air Line Pilots
Association. II. Fitness Institute. III. Title.
RC1063.S73   613.7   78-27361

ISBN 0-440-03670-4

Contents

The author wishes to thank Doug MacLennan of the Fitness Institute for his generous contribution of time and expertise during the writing of this book, and for his work in developing the self-assessment and recommended fitness programs that are presented in the manual.

Prologue

To get off the ground, all pilots must have regular medical checkups. Whether they fly for commercial airlines, for the armed forces or purely for pleasure, all pilots are concerned that sooner or later they may fail their medical. Once grounded, many never fly again. For a professional pilot, grounding means an enormous loss of income and a doubtful personal future. Since the incidence of grounding increases with age, the middle-aged pilot may suddenly find himself without a job with his self-image shattered.

Heart disease is the cause of 60 per cent of groundings. Other causes include mental instability, a dependence on drugs to combat a chronic illness, and diseases which are likely to interfere with the safe handling of an aircraft at any altitude throughout a prolonged or difficult fight. Disorders which cause grounding are sensory (such as poor eyesight and deafness), motor (spinal diseases, joint disorders and muscle weakness), psychiatric (anxiety states and depression), those which may cause sudden incapacitation (heart disease and seizure disorders), and those which may cause gradual incapacitation (hypoglycemia, chronic alcoholism, leukemia).

Many causes for grounding, particularly heart disease, are related to a neglect of physical fitness. The best way for a pilot to keep flying is for him to practise good fitness and health habits both in the air and on the ground. Unfortunately, professional pilots face unique stresses which militate against a high level of personal fitness: irregular hours of work and sleep, long periods of sitting, and a constantly changing environment and diet.

This book describes these problems and how to overcome them. Commissioned by the Canadian Air Line Pilots Association for use by airline pilots, the book is also suitable for private pilots and anyone else seeking advice on the important topic of physical fitness. It has been written with the cooperation of the Fitness Institute in Toronto, and the testing procedures, exercise programs and general fitness recommendations are based upon methods that have been used successfully at the institute over the past fourteen years.

*Canadian Pilot's
Fitness Manual*

1

Fear of Grounding

What the fool does in the end, the wise man does in the
beginning — ANCIENT PROVERB

In 1972 Don Fisher, an Air Canada DC–8 captain was grounded
by the Canadian Ministry of Transport. In a routine medical check-
up, his electrocardiogram revealed irregular heart action. At 42,
Don found himself suddenly discouraged and depressed, his future
gloomy. Flying was both his career and his hobby; he had been
president of a national and a community flying club.

"I wanted to be a pilot," he said. "Some pilots sort of fall into this
kind of work, but I wanted it. Although I was grounded, I was
optimistic that I could get my licence back."

Don scrambled. He went to the Shute Institute in London, Ontario, to find out about the reported benefits of Vitamin E, and to the
Mayo Clinic in Rochester, Minnesota, to have a thorough heart
examination. With his doctor's approval, he joined the Fitness
Institute in Toronto, started a planned exercise program and soon
lost 16 kilograms. After seven months of exercising, dieting, and
visiting medical people, the Ministry agreed that he was again fit to
fly. Today Don maintains a high level of fitness and his airline pilot's
licence.

Fitness programs have helped others. One story concerns Captain Arthur Yarrington who in the mid-1960s suffered a heart attack
and was grounded by the U.S. Air Force. Under care of fitness
expert Dr. Ken Cooper, Captain Yarrington started walking and

then running, eventually achieving distances up to 40 kilometres a day. He may have been the first U.S. pilot to be restored to flying status after having a heart condition.

Some airlines report an annual grounding rate of about 1 per cent. Medical disqualification during the first two years of a pilot's career is a rarity, but after the age of 45 there is a dramatic increase in the number with serious disease. Fewer than 50 per cent of pilots are flying at 60.

"We average about three letters per working day from those who have been denied the privileges of a pilot's licence on medical grounds," said Bill Peppler, director of the Canadian Owners and Pilots Association. "In most cases had the 'victim' been made aware of the necessity of being careful about his health ten years ago and taken appropriate action, then in all probability he would still be flying today."

Because groundings increase with pilot age, the majority of those grounded have reached a time in life when it's difficult to find other employment. Some have the good fortune to continue employment with their companies as simulator instructors or office workers; others are forced onto the street. Estimates of the cost for training a senior airline pilot range up to $500,000, and for a military pilot, up to $750,000. Whether paid by the airlines, the military or the pilot himself, or a combination of these sources, it's a poor investment if a career is cut short by grounding.

What happens to the permanently grounded pilot? Airline pilots can insure themselves against grounding — up to $120,000. Bush pilots and other commercial and private pilots aren't eligible for this scheme. The principal sum is paid one year after the pilot is declared permanently grounded and attempts for reinstatement have been unsuccessful. The Aviation Insurance Agency of the United States, which also serves Canadian and Australian commercial airline pilots, reduces the principal to be paid to each pilot as he grows older. For instance, an annual premium of $576 buys a 39-year-old pilot $100,000 of coverage while a slightly higher premium gains the 59-year-old pilot only $2,000 of insurance. Before the company settles a claim, it often sends a grounded pilot to the Mayo Clinic for examination and treatment from aerospace medical specialists to find out if his health can be restored. Convinced that it is less expensive to prevent than cure the grounding disease, the Aviation

Insurance Agency publishes an excellent monthly, *Aviation Medical Bulletin*, with advice on health problems. And most pilots have a positive desire to preserve their good health. As Air Canada pilot Sam Gilmour says, "We're not exactly hypochondriacs, but without our health we are birds with clipped wings. Fitness is our economic highway."

Yet, despite the universal fear of grounding, some pilots refuse to take any action to reduce the risk. A few are fatalistic about their careers and take no measures to prevent the possibility of being grounded. One Air Canada pilot said that if he had read the fitness literature, followed exercise and diet programs, and constantly worried about his health, he would be more nervous and unhealthy than he is now. While it is remotely possible to become ill by trying too hard to avoid illness, far more pilots become ill and are grounded because they don't try hard enough. Some make pathetic attempts by living perfectly healthy lives — for the last week or two before their medicals! If they have borderline health, this practice may put off the inevitable for one or two medicals. Some visit their family doctors before their air medicals for advice, if not magic, to boost their health above the acceptable level. But "cramming" for a medical test isn't as effective as last-minute studying for an examination. The body adjusts more slowly than the brain. The body will rebel with sickness, tiredness or soreness if a lifestyle adjustment is forced upon it too rapidly. And fitness cramming can also be dangerous, particularly if the pilot is suffering a serious, undetected illness. A sudden flurry of push-ups or a 6-kilometre jog can trigger a heart attack in an unfit person.

The ominous consequences of being grounded don't become apparent to many pilots until it actually happens to them. And then it can be too late. The offending disease is often irreversible or cannot be controlled. Even during their flying career, some pilots start a second career, to have something to fall back on. For most, the second job is never as good as the first. Aviation is their adventure, addiction, an escape from urban pollution and the business world: it's a pleasant, highly paid avocation. No insurance money or second job can make up for the losses of grounding.

2 The Medical

Too many men can take no time to be well, but can
always take time to be ill.

With evidence that an existing or impending mental or physical
disability will reduce a pilot's competence and therefore endanger
the public's safety, air transportation authorities around the world
have been granted a mandate to ground medically unfit pilots. When
international air traffic expanded rapidly during World War Two,
member countries of the International Civil Aviation Organization
(ICAO) met to discuss pilot medical standards. Recognizing that air
travel was drastically shrinking the world, air regulations were
bound to be more universal than automobile or train travel standards. All contracting states agreed at a convention in Chicago in
1944 to impose medical regulations in accordance with standards
and recommended practices of medicine now outlined in the International Civil Aviation Organization *Manual of Civil Aviation
Medicine*. Many countries draft their own regulations based on local
needs, but all subscribe to the minimum standards so that the
medical stability of a pilot who regularly crosses international bor-
ders is not subject to separate licensing in each contracting state.

Because air accidents attract so much public attention, air medical standards tend to be rigid and conservative. They reflect the
acute public desire for air safety, but cannot be so unreasonably
tough that they are successfully challenged in the courts. Canada,
along with 140 other nations, closely heeds these international medical standards.

The Canadian Ministry of Transport may cancel or suspend a pilot licence if a pilot is thought to be "incompetent or physically unfit to exercise the rights and privileges" afforded in his licence. Medical officers can't be available before and during each flight, so a pilot must assess his own condition and shall not fly if he is aware that he has a physical disability that might render him unable to meet the requirements as to physical condition for the issue or renewal of his licence. The *Canadian Personnel Licensing Handbook* explains that the aim of the medical is to discover if the airline transport pilot licence applicant has any abnormality or injury that is likely to "interfere with the safe handling of an aircraft at any altitude throughout a prolonged or difficult flight or may reasonably be expected within the period of the licence to make the applicant unfit to exercise the privileges of the licence applied for or held."

Specifically, "the applicant shall not suffer from any disease or disability which renders him liable to become unable to handle an aircraft safely," and "shall have no established medical history or clinical diagnosis which, according to accredited medical conclusion, would render the applicant unable to exercise safely the privileges of his licence." The verbiage is not so lengthy for the private pilot, but the message is the same.

The most important rationale for aviation regulations, including the strict medical examination of pilots, is safety. Totally safe airborne aircraft and pilots are an impossible ideal, although there are indications that aviation is getting closer to that ideal. United States Air Force statistics show a drop in major accidents, from 6.7 per 100,000 flying hours in 1960 to 3 per 100,000 in 1970. A recent study revealed the death rate in commercial aircraft accidents in the United States has dropped to one thirty-fifth of what it was some thirty years ago. Commercial jet travel is fifteen times safer per passenger mile than driving a car. The risk for private pilots is four times greater than commercial pilots.

One essential question is, "What relation exists between poor health and air safety?" Some suggest the relationship is flimsy and unprovable. They would abolish air medicals. The Aircraft Owners and Pilots Association of the United States, in criticizing a government call for tighter medical regulations in 1976, said the odds against fatal accidents being caused by medical problems which can be diagnosed in advance are at least one hundred million to one. The government reported on six hundred accidents over a ten-year period, some of which might have been avoided by stricter medicals. In fifty-eight incidents cardiovascular problems were present, but the report conceded that only nineteen of these could have been detected beforehand. In the October 31, 1975, issue of the *American Journal of Cardiology,* Captain Roderic Gilstrap, vice-president of the Air Line Pilots Association, said that "no fatal accident of a scheduled civilian jet air-carrier in the United States has been attributed to a pilot's medical incapacitation from any cause." Medical authorities must alter standards for the world of DC–10s and not be mired in the vanquished world of DC–3s, he said. They should know about the cockpit environment of a modern airliner, "with its complex instrumentation and numerous safety systems, including the human beings functioning as part of the operational fail-safe crew." He criticized "lower level" physicians for taking the easy way out by rejecting the borderline pilot. "We find intolerable the unwarranted and unnecessary grounding of pilots . . . from an incompetent evaluation," he added.

But even the most enlightened critic will admit that some method is necessary to screen the unhealthy pilot because he is more likely to suffer sudden incapacitation (such as an in-air heart attack) or a reduced capacity to operate his aircraft (for example, poor vision) which would lower his ability to make rapid and sane judgments.

What about larger aircraft guided by a pilot and co-pilot? The chance of having two pilots who have been declared medically fit becoming incapacitated simultaneously for independent medical reasons is bordering on the impossible. But the medical does serve a purpose: it reduces the risk of the pilot-in-command being incapacitated at the critical moments of take-off or landing, an accumulated time of approximately 15 hours over a six-month period for the average airline pilot. During simulation training, airline pilots are trained to detect incapacitation in their partner pilot and immediately take the controls.

Accident investigators conclude that 90 per cent of accidents are caused by human factors. Pilot judgment is a more crucial consideration in air safety than sudden incapacitation. But predicting that a pilot will display dangerous behaviour or judgment in the sky is an almost impossible task for medical evaluators. Each case of an applicant with criminal, psychotic or abnormal behavioural record is judged on its merits. Transport Canada's aircraft accident reports disclose a large number occur because private and commercial pilots have chosen to fly into deteriorating weather conditions. Some bad judgments by private pilots have been traced to fatigue or alcohol. Dazzling advances have been made since the Wright brothers' original flight, particularly in the past fifteen years, to improve aircraft safety features. Unfortunately, the human machine is locked into the evolutionary process and isn't capable of a similar glittering progress. If the totally healthy pilot has difficulty understanding and handling an aircraft, the job for an unhealthy one is even more ominous. The judgment of a healthy pilot is not blurred by the discomfort or depression that often accompanies the state of unfitness and ill health.

Air medical regulations don't demand a high level of pilot physical fitness. They are worded in the negative: a pilot shall *not* have specific medical problems. "A pilot can be unfit and overweight and still qualify for his licence," said Captain Bob Dodds of Toronto, an Air Canada pilot and chairman of the Canadian Air Line Pilots Association Aeromedical Committee. "But a pilot's unfit condition will often lead to medical problems. His unfitness starts a chain of events that eventually grounds him."

In Canada a pilot must take a medical examination from a specially appointed doctor. Medicals are required every two years for private pilots under 40 and every year for those over 40. Airline pilots are checked every six months. Some doctors and pilots suggest that examinations are too frequent for those under 40 and not often enough for those over 40 and 50. Approximately 10 per cent of the sixty thousand applications processed annually in Canada are "borderline." About six hundred difficult cases are referred each year to the Medical Review Board's seven physicians in Ottawa. Pilots who are unhappy with the Review Board's recommendations can appeal to the Medical Appeal Panel which has four private consultants who meet four times a year. The advice of medical experts can be rejected by the Ministry Licensing Branch. The delicate issue is to decide at which point the pilot's medical risk is too high. A group to be known as the Aviation Safety Appeal Board is being established by Transport Canada to hear appeals from pilots who believe they have been treated unfairly by ministry inspectors.

Aeromedical officers say they are on the side of the pilot. The late

Dr. Roy Chatterton, an Ontario air medical examiner, told a Canadian Owners and Pilots Association conference on flight fitness in 1976 that the examiners' chief aim is to "get you to fly and give you the highest rating possible." At the same conference, Dr. Ian Anderson, senior civil aviation medical consultant in Canada, advised pilots to seek out examiners who themselves are pilots. The International Civil Aviation Organization standards make the same point: "[Medical] examiners should possess practical knowledge and experience of the environmental conditions in which the holders of professional licences and ratings carry out their duties. An accumulated total of at least 10 hours per year of flight-deck time might be considered desirable." Those ultimately responsible for medical licensing sometimes must decide between facing an irate grounded pilot or the possibility of a coroner's jury probing why a now-dead pilot wasn't kept out of the air.

Dr. Anderson considers that it is possible to predict pilot risk with some accuracy by using the same mathematical formula used to judge the reliability of an aircraft. Engineers calculate minimum safety levels of aircraft components by reviewing their breakdown rate, measured in terms of one default for each several million flying hours. By using the human breakdown rate, based on such medical data as the Framingham Study on heart disease, each pilot can be judged on his medical and family history and personal lifestyle to determine his reliability rating. While Anderson concedes it is impossible to reach perfection in such calculations, he said "the unexpected but excellent fit of the coronary risk with aircraft system reliability is encouraging. It can be observed, for example, that the post-coronary patient with his average mortality of 5 per cent per year would probably fall outside the standards. Although the statistical and epidemiological gymnastics necessary to achieve such a comparison preclude its use for individual licensing purposes, it provides a crude guideline for prediction of the borderline or 'intermediate risk' pilot."

Dr. John Quinlan of the Medical Appeal Panel in Ottawa said his group makes "educated guesses" on the chance of an appellant with a questionable medical condition meeting with disaster in an aircraft. To guarantee objectivity in judging borderline cases, each pilot is known by number, not name. There is no organized follow-up on those who successfully appeal, but no serious incidents involving a pilot who has gone through the appeal process is known to the panel, said Quinlan.

Departures from International Civil Aviation Organization standards are permitted if medical authorities are satisfied that flight safety isn't jeopardized. Special restrictions can be placed on licences. An applicant finding himself unfit for one duty may qualify for another, such as flight navigator or engineer. Or the pilot may be restricted to co-pilot duty. One condition may be that the pilot must submit to a medical or a pertinent portion of a medical more often than normally required. Borderline problems are often referred to medical specialists, and in-flight or simulated flight testing is sometimes used to determine the degree of debilitation. International Civil Aviation Organization standards include descriptions of procedures to determine the severity of handicap from physical deformities (the loss of a limb or limbs), visual and hearing defects, and colour blindness.

The Appeal Panel in Canada is all the more careful in its decisions, knowing they can be used as precedents binding on the outcome of similar appeals in future. Two of the most challenging kinds of cases involve appellants who use drugs to control an existing illness and those who have alleged psychological disturbances. Investigations by air medical authorities are often hampered by pilots' personal physicians who believe they are protecting their patients by refusing to disclose certain medical facts. These non-aero physicians reason, with some validity, that disclosure itself would be one more factor contributing to the patient's illness, if it is, for instance, hypertension or psychiatric.

Dr. Earl Carter of the Mayo Clinic said that no area of occupational medicine offers a greater challenge to the "diagnostic and therapeutic acumen" of doctors than aviation medicine. The most difficult chore for doctors is to accurately assess the pilot applicant's motivation to fly or to be grounded. Physical handicaps themselves can heighten a pilot's motivation to fly – to show the world that he's just as good, probably better, than healthier men. Persons with severe handicaps have earned pilot's licences. The medical examination obviously cannot measure the positive human qualities such as desire, courage and mechanical skills.

There is good evidence that medical licensing procedures in Canada have improved substantially in the past few years, but because the decision on who is fit to fly will always be a matter of human opinion, the medical will continue to be one of the most controversial topics in aviation.

Besides making the skies safer, medical standards force pilots to be more conscious of preventive medicine and the need for good personal fitness habits. If a pilot fails to stay healthy, an intermediate step can be taken to ground him pending further investigation of his disease or disability. The scare of temporary grounding often pushes a pilot to change his lifestyle. The immediate improvement in his health usually renders further investigation unnecessary.

Let's turn now to an examination of diseases and disabilities which can ground pilots.

3 Common Grounding Diseases

Most pilots don't wear out – they rust out!

1. THE HEART AND CIRCULATORY SYSTEM

Among the stacks of accident reports provided to pilots in Canada are a few pinpointing the cause as "heart attack." One described a private pilot in a float plane that dived 45 metres straight down into water moments after taking off. The pilot had suffered a fatal heart attack. In another case, an airline transport pilot in a Piper PA–23 struck some trees, cutting a 260-metre swath before it stopped in an inverted position. The post-mortem revealed the pilot had advanced atherosclerotic heart disease. He had been a hard worker and heavy smoker, and although he complained of chest pains, his medical showed no significant illnesses. His electrocardiogram was normal.

Three to six Canadian private pilots die each year in aircraft accidents after suffering incapacitation from a heart attack. For obvious reasons, multiple crew aircraft aren't subject to the same level of risk. But when sudden incapacitation does occur in commercial airlines, the results can be tragic. A study of seventeen countries from 1961 to 1969 revealed five accidents involving 148 deaths among passengers and crews, all caused by pilot incapacitation.

Unfortunately, heart disease doesn't always bless the pilot-victim and his medical appraiser with early identifiable symptoms. It can strike even the outwardly healthy pilot without warning, causing unconsciousness, confusion, amnesia and sudden death. Researchers have described "silent" ischemic heart disease as "by far the most important clinical problem in aviation medicine." One study of 150 active pilots over 40 years of age showed about 15 per cent had some evidence of heart disease; but none had overt symptoms.

Because the devastation of heart and circulatory diseases often occurs suddenly, many of these diseases if found in pilots are disqualifying. A discussion of each would be too lengthy for inclusion here, but in general the symptoms may include unusual fatigue, loss of exercise capacity, chest pain, and increasingly frequent heart palpitations. High blood pressure, high resting and exercise pulse rates, and an abnormal condition of blood vessels in the eye also offer the medical examiner important clues. While an electrocardiogram cannot always detect heart disease, it is sensitive to changes in the electric activity of the heart which, if monitored over a period of months or years, are an important indication of the presence of degenerative diseases of the heart, particularly of the coronary arteries. In conjunction with the electrocardiogram, cardiologists employ a stress test: stepping up on a box, riding a stationary bicycle ergometer, or walking or running on an inclined treadmill.

Some "internal" methods of detecting heart disease, such as arterial catheterization, may offer a more accurate diagnosis, but they are too complex, time-consuming and costly for mass screening. A new method of assessing heart abnormalities involves injecting protein containing a trace of radioactivity into a vein and then reading the behaviour of the radioactive substance in the heart during exercise. This method is safer and less expensive than other forms of angiography or cardiac picture-taking.

It is not always coronary disease that causes momentary unconsciousness, confusion or amnesia in flight. High altitudes, disturbances to the central nervous system, or severe emotional stress can deprive the brain of the necessary supply of oxygen. During World War Two a study was made of five hundred Royal Air Force pilots who had been stricken with a loss of consciousness. Only 31 per cent of the men were found to have cardiovascular problems, and only 7 per cent of that number were identified as having organic heart disease severe enough to cause a loss of consciousness. Some 42 per cent of the cases of lost consciousness were related to emotional reasons.

In the western world coronary heart disease is the major cause of death for men over 40 and women over 50. Before men reach 45, accidents are the chief cause, and later in life, cancer is the main killer, but overall, heart disease has the dubious distinction of "out-killing" wars, revolution, natural disasters, accidents and cancer. It is the cause of approximately one half of all deaths in North America.

A report on "Aviation Cardiology in Canada" appearing in the *American Journal of Cardiology* in October 1975 contained a calculation that seven or eight airline pilots and twenty-two to twenty-three private pilots could be expected to have a "coronary event" each year. It noted that in 1971 five airline pilots and two senior commercial pilots had on-ground heart attacks. Five of the ten cases described in the article ended in sudden death, two immediately after landing and one shortly before take-off. The ten cardiac pilots were of ages ranging from 37 to 64.

Of growing concern is that more men at a younger age are heart attack victims. Some doctors report that attacks on younger men seem to be more severe, often fatal. While modern medical research has been able to conquer a myriad of once crippling ailments, heart disease, along with cancer, remains the central reason why life expectancy has not improved over the past few decades.

Besides the human brain – the most complex and mysterious apparatus in the known universe – the heart is a source of wonder. In the average person it beats about 72 times each minute. The average heart will beat 4,320 times every hour, 104,000 every day, 38 million every year and 2.7 billion in the average life span of 70 years! It is not permitted the luxury of weekends off, holidays, not a moment's rest. Yet for all its involuntary work, it rarely complains or causes pain. (It's interesting to note that a heart rate reduced by exercise to two-thirds of an average rate will beat 900 million fewer times in a human life.)

The heart is divided into four chambers, a twin pump taking dark (oxygen-poor) blood from the veins, pumping it into the lungs, drawing the bright red (oxygen-rich) blood back into the heart and then distributing it to the rest of the body. More than one gallon of blood is circulated through the body every minute. The oxygen, hormones, and restorative food substances circulate to the brain, digestive tract, kidneys, liver, reproductive system and muscles, including the tireless heart muscle itself. The heart is the administrative centre of a complex transport, waste disposal and temperature control system, delivering oxygen (that provides mobility), and exporting carbon dioxide from the body through the lungs. The heart muscle is served by left and right coronary arteries whose smallest branches interconnect. The long fibres of the heart muscle contract rhythmically, the tempo increasing with the demand of physical work or mental stress. Because it is an indirect indicator of the heart muscle's demand for oxygen, the pulse rate, taken during a flight task, can be used as a measure of the cardio vascular load being experienced. The heart's capacity as a pump is three to four times greater than its idling or basal rate. Normal pilot routines will not dig so deeply into heart's reserves. The monitoring of pulse rates of healthy pilots during take-offs and landings, however, reveal rates close to age-predicted maximums. Other cardiovascular stresses on pilots are sometimes caused by loss of oxygen in pressurized aircraft and by G-forces in crop-dusting and aerobatic flying.

Heart capacity is limited by the number of beats it can maintain and the volume of blood it ejects with each beat, which together are known as cardiac output. Exercise can improve cardiac output by gradually increasing the per stroke volume of blood.

A major cause of ischemic heart disease is the accumulation of fatty deposits, atherosclerotic plaques, which harden on the coronary artery walls. This build-up may be observed in arteries in other parts of the body, but when it occurs around the heart the consequences can be fatal. As plaques increase in size, partially blocking the flow of blood to the heart muscle, anginal pain may be felt, particularly when the heart workload is increased. "Angina pectoris" normally disappears when exertion subsides. An enlarged plaque may rupture, block the narrowed passage, and shut off blood supply. The portion of the heart muscle that is denied blood quickly dies. If the damage is too great, the heart stops. If the victim survives, he is weakened while a radical adjustment is being made to his damaged heart. During the next weeks the damaged area becomes scar tissue. The severity of the damage and the presence of the disease in the remaining coronary arteries will indicate the patient's chances of returning to a normal life.

Another complication of coronary artery disease can be an ineffective stroke volume. Blood fails to reach the brain and in minutes the patient dies. Coronary plaques can also simply wear down the heart's efficiency over several years so that eventually it can't function properly and fluid begins to congest the lungs, liver, abdomen and feet. Ultimately, the heart can no longer perform. Once the disease has reached an advanced state, it may require only an immediate jolt of exercise or emotion to bring on a full-blown heart attack. It can be a lack of sleep, a fight with the boss, changing a tire, a weekend with too much booze and dancing, indigestion, a viral infection, or the first game of touch football in four years.

For pilots, it is obvious that the emotional strain of landing an aircraft in bad weather carries the essential ingredients for triggering a heart attack if the pilot has advanced heart disease. It could also be argued that if a heart attack is going to happen during a flight, it is most likely during a stressful landing.

Doctors are unable to trace the exact cause of heart disease. Instead they use the term "risk factor," many of which are associated with the good life: overeating, over-stress, and under-exercising. Men in the 40 to 59 age group in affluent industrial countries are eight times more susceptible to heart disease than those living in developing countries.

One highly publicized risk factor of heart disease is the over-abundance of cholesterol in our diet. The average North American needs only about one quarter to one half of the cholesterol he consumes. But it's not a simple matter of avoiding certain foods such as milk and egg products. Researchers in recent years have discovered that the substances that actually transport cholesterol in the bloodstream are a strong indicator of risk. Some may cause heart disease; however, others, known as high density lipoproteins (HDL's)), are believed responsible for cleansing unneeded cholesterol from artery walls. While an absence of adequate levels of HDL's is found in about 40 per cent of young men with heart disease, a Stanford University study of middle-aged men showed their HDL levels improved with running long distances. Dieting and avoiding large quantities of saturated fats apparently increase HDL levels.

Another risk factor is alcohol, which is high in calories. A few drinks each day can destroy the benefits of dieting. If you insist on drinking, insist on very little.

Smoking, too, is a risk factor. It is associated with so many diseases, including heart problems, it's a wonder that millions of people have the habit. But then so few addictions are rational. Men under 65 who smoke have a 100 per cent greater chance of contracting heart disease than non-smokers. Those who inhale elevate their pulse by as many as 20 beats a minute, and raise their blood pressure. Smoking causes constriction of the blood vessels in the extremities, leading to lowered peripheral circulation and increased workload on the heart.

Another alleged risk factor that leaves a wake of unanswered questions is behaviour characterized by tension and hostility. Dr. Meyer Friedman of San Francisco traced the medical histories of more than 3,000 men over fifteen years and concluded that a majority of heart disease victims are ambitious, compulsive, highly aggressive and competitive, rarely satisfied, impatient and eternally watching a clock. Spouses and friends encourage them to relax and enjoy life, but they put it off for another day, a day that ironically never arrives. The stress produces a high blood cholesterol count, a flow of adrenalin-like substances in the blood, and a reduction of some needed hormones. Dr. Friedman distinguishes between a person's personality (it can't be fundamentally changed) and behaviour (which can be changed). Is Dr. Friedman advocating preventive medicine for heart disease, or promoting a life philosophy? He believes medicine and philosophy are closely linked and is critical of the medical profession for its apparent preoccupation with statistics, measurements and physical explanations for questions that find their best answers in the human soul. Heart-destroying tensions are caused when people prefer "having" to "being," he says.

The chief risk factor in coronary heart disease, however, is hypertension (high blood pressure). Pilots suffering hypertension or treating their hypertension with drugs are usually grounded, depending on the severity of the disease. Approximately thirty million citizens of Canada and the United States are hypertensive. Sometimes described as the quiet killer, not only is it linked to heart disease, it is also the chief cause of strokes — that is, the rupture of a blood vessel in the brain. Blood pressure is the force exerted on vessel walls by the heart pumping blood through the circulation system, an estimated 60,000 miles of vessels. Without this pressure, blood couldn't reach any vital areas of the body. High blood pressure increases the workload on the heart and accelerates the aging process of the circulation system. Among the numerous complications caused by high blood pressure are kidney disease, internal hemorrhages and damage to the eyes. Hypertension is the single most important measurement used by insurance companies to predict life expectancy. The higher the pressure, the shorter the life expectancy.

Blood pressure is recorded as two figures. The higher figure is the systolic pressure – the force exerted in the vessels as the heart muscle is contracting. The lower figure is the diastolic blood pressure between pulse beats when the heart is momentarily relaxed and filling with blood. There is no agreed pressure line dividing a normal from a hypertensive person. Some doctors are concerned when a patient is 130/90. Others won't suggest treatment until it reaches 180/110. Blood pressure readings of 140/90 to 160/95 are generally in the marginal high pressure range. Approximately 15 per cent of the adult population in North America is in this category. Pressures above 160/95 are usually defined as "definite hypertensive." Borderline hypertensives often maintain a similiar reading for much of their lives, while those with more severe pressure usually find it rising from year to year. A study of four million life insurance policy holders in the United States over a nineteen-year period ending in 1953 revealed that men with systolic pressures exceeding 198 and diastolic pressures of 118 or more are seven times more likely to suffer an early death than persons with a normal reading. Persons with low readings, such as 110/70 could expect to live a longer life.

In Canada, a person with a diastolic reading of slightly less than 100 may qualify for a private, but not a commercial licence, subject to a yearly check-up. Each case is given individual scrutiny, heeding an applicant's medical history, age, weight and other factors.

Stress can increase blood pressure. This places the borderline hypertensive pilot facing his medical in double jeopardy because the worry about finding his blood pressure too high may raise it to the disqualification category. Even if the doctor is friendly and talks about the weather or golf, the pilot knows it's the unspoken, the reading, that counts. One research team found that readings taken at home are usually lower than in the doctor's office. Readings also vary according to the time of day, activity and other circumstances. Average pressure can drop by 20 to 50 per cent during sleep. Some

U.S. pilots meditate to reduce their blood pressure by five or more points. Medical authorities are concerned that hypertensive pilots are using meditation to beat the screening process.

Pilots under prolonged periods of stress will discover that they are unable to bring their blood pressure back to its previous level even when they consciously relax. Hypertension can be alleviated, but it requires time, planning and personal discipline. A traditional antidote is to lose weight. Obesity is a common condition associated with hypertension; mortality is considerably higher for hypertensives who are also fat. Drugs are a popular treatment for high blood pressure. One family of drugs works against the nerve and body chemicals that constrict blood vessels. Another kind, diuretics, allow the body and its blood to retain a lower volume of fluid, thus relieving blood pressure. Unfortunately for hypertensive pilots, many drugs cause sleepiness and dizziness and are therefore banned. More medical researchers are viewing drug therapy for mild hypertension as artificial patching. They are favouring lifestyle modification: losing weight; reducing intake of salt, animal fats and alcohol; stopping smoking; and relaxing and exercising more.

It is impossible to isolate any one risk factor such as hypertension and say it is to blame for all heart disease. A man who smokes and drinks heavily is usually less inclined to participate in regular physical activity; an obese person is more likely to have a higher than average blood cholesterol count, possibly high blood pressure, and lack physical fitness. Many protections against heart disease involve the word "don't." Don't eat too much. Don't load up on high cholesterol foods. Don't drink. Don't smoke. Don't stress yourself at work. Just don't!

The lack of fitness is one risk factor that has a positive antidote. *Do* exercises. If some of the activities outlined later in this book are done conscientiously, many other risk factors will disappear. For instance, exercising may lower your blood pressure, aid your diet and strengthen your heart muscle.

2. PSYCHOLOGICAL FACTORS

While it appears that strong links exist between physical fitness and the absence of cardiovascular problems, the association of fitness to mental health is difficult to demonstrate. There is substance to the dictum "a strong body means a strong mind," but discovering exactly how it works, pinpointing the causal connectors, can take investigators into the realm of opinion and speculation. But some factors are difficult to deny: physical activity is an outlet, a release for frustrations and anxieties common in our complex world; and being in good physical shape gives a person a sense of well-being and confidence which can't be achieved if the body is frail and/or ill.

Psychological fitness is the pilot's ability to make choices and safely navigate in a flying environment that isn't beyond his skill capacity. It is the readiness to overcome unexpected hazards and act coolly when others would panic. All categories of licence-holders or applicants are disqualified from flying if they have a psychosis, dependence on alcohol or drugs, any personality disorder (particularly if severe enough to have repeatedly resulted in overt acts), or a mental abnormality or neurosis. To be grounded the "accredited medical conclusion" must be that the pilot is unable to safely exercise the privileges of the licence.

It is almot impossible for licensing authorities to accurately assess the ability of pilots to make correct judgments while in flight. One medical examiner said he learns more from an informal chat with a pilot than from pulse and blood pressure readings. This doctor, himself a pilot, asks himself when interviewing a pilot, "Would I feel safe flying with this man?" An interview with a prospective pilot can reveal key traits such as a borderline low intelligence or an advanced degree of irresponsibility, reasons for the examiner to request more thorough testing. Asking a person to explain why he flies may bring maladjustments to the surface, but they are more likely to remain hidden in the short interview.

It could be argued that aviation medicals over-emphasize detection of the physical and under-emphasize detection of the mental deficiencies of pilots. Despite recent advances, psychology remains a more subjective and nebulous discipline than physiology. The manifestation of a mental problem, if it is ever revealed, may not show up for several years, and then may appear as a fatal crash or demonstration of hazardous or reckless flying. Subtle forms of mental deficiency may be evident only in the subject's inability to make realistic judgments in the cockpit.

The pilot's problem may be that he rates his capabilities too highly and under-estimates the dangers around him. It is incorrect to describe bad judgment as mental illness, but if it causes death, somehow the expression "bad judgment" seems too casual. Pilot alertness may be retarded by psychiatric or organic mental deficiencies. Milder forms of psychiatric problems, such as neuroses and personality disorders, are more prevalent and difficult for aviation medicos to deal with than severe forms, such as psychoses. Symptoms of neurosis are familiar to most people: anxiety, headaches, sleeplessness, and depression. In advanced psychiatric illness, the symptoms are incapacitating and the view of reality may be distorted. A crippling state of anxiety caused by family or financial problems occurs only rarely among pilots. More common are phobic anxieties which may result from such situations as flying in clouds or at high altitudes.

The greatest number of air accidents in Canada and the United States are caused by pilots making mental errors; and many involve a brash private pilot losing an in-air joust with the weather. Transport Canada reports are revealing in their repetitive description of air accidents: "The pilot attempted visual flight in mountainous terrain in poor weather"; "Pilot continued Visual Flight Regulations in deteriorating weather." In the United States in 1969, for instance, there were 4,767 general aviation accidents, including 647 crashes that ended with fatalities; about 25 per cent were caused by pilots trying to continue visual flight in adverse weather.

Dr. Louis Fabre of the University of Texas told the 1975 Congress of Aviation Space Medicine in Acapulco that pilots, like other humans, are irrational. They may have high intelligence quotients and be totally aware of the mistakes they are making as they are making them! While training and supervision militate against making gross errors, Dr. Fabre said pilots have a problem (irrationality) for which there is no apparent solution. The safety systems in multi-crew aircraft reduce the risk of pilot error, but a man flying by himself is a risk to himself, he said.

3. ALCOHOL

No matter how physically fit a pilot may be, a few ounces of alcohol can make him unfit to fly. Alcohol interferes with pilot judgment;

addiction to it is a ticket to permanent grounding. An alcoholic must be on the wagon for a minimum of one year before regaining his professional pilot's licence and then he must continue to visit a psychiatrist every six months for the following two years with proof of complete abstinence. A single relapse will mean permanent grounding.

Fortunately, the recorded incidence of alcoholism among professional pilots is less than one in every five thousand per year. The actual level is probably higher, but afflicted pilots and, in some cases, their companies, refuse to label over-drinking as alcoholism. The extremely low incidence of alcoholism is somewhat surprising because all classes of pilots often face temptations to drink. Airline pilots may want to drink to help them sleep or to combat boredom, fatigue or irregular scheduling during a stopover. Flight crews working in distant outposts may look to drink to relieve loneliness. Private pilots may be tempted to drink socially at the flying club.

But to heed regulations and maintain necessary skill levels and the onerous responsibility of piloting, these temptations must be resisted. Most airline pilots would not dare to drink an hour or two before flight duty, although tales are told of a few who have stayed up drinking the night before a morning flight. A few years ago any airline pilot who drank at the wrong time was treated as a discipline case — usually suspended for a short time. Today the problem is being treated as more of a sickness. At least one Canadian airline has a "quiet-running" professional standards advisory committee which works in the background assisting pilots to overcome a variety of personal difficulties, including alcohol abuse.

In the absence of such policing and pressure, there are indications that more private pilots flirt with alcohol before flying. A U.S. study of 1,345 fatal general aviation accidents in the past decade revealed that 8.7 per cent of pilots and 4.6 per cent of passengers had alcohol levels considered intoxicating. Another 10.7 per cent of pilots and 3.5 per cent of passengers had traceable but not intoxicating levels.

Flying is more complex than driving an automobile because air routes are three dimensional and roads only two. Even in direct, smooth-weather flights, the pilot must make hundreds of decisions rapidly. A lessening of control and concentration caused by alcohol can be disastrous, as shown in Transport Canada's thick file on accidents.

Drinking gives the impression of stimulation, confidence, good feeling; but the alcohol, no matter whether it's beer, wine or hard liquor, is a depressant, sedating the central nervous system. The speed at which alcohol enters the bloodstream is slowed by the presence of food, particularly fatty food, in the stomach and lower digestive tract. But when it gets into the blood, alcohol lays siege to areas of the brain, depriving them of adequate volumes of oxygen and nerve impulses. Adversely affected are reaction time, comprehension, vision, hearing, logical thought, the power of self-assessment, memory and physical coordination. Alcohol also induces fatigue and sleep. Behaviour is altered and often what the intoxicated pilot believes is courageous flying is merely elevated irresponsibility.

A private pilot may argue that a small amount of alcohol does not impair his judgment. He shouldn't assume that good habits developed in training and flying experience will help him negotiate when under the influence of drink, strong or weak. Quite the opposite; these refined skills are the first to be affected. The detrimental effects of alcohol on pilot judgment increase with altitude. One drink at 10,000 feet has the same impact as two or three at sea level.

In the next section we will explore the various pilot stresses. One that deserves mention here is the stress of a hangover. While the hangover itself is not an intoxicated condition, the weary, hungover pilot is not well equipped to handle routine flight chores and other stresses. Aviation authorities in both Canada and the United States demand that a pilot wait at least eight hours after one drink before flying and recommend that a sensible bottle-to-throttle time is twelve hours. After heavy drinking it takes up to two days for the body to return to normal. For instance, the prolonged effect of alcohol on the balance mechanism of the inner ear can cause random movements of the eyeball, making it difficult to read an instrument panel or spot a nearby airborne plane.

4. DRUGS

Rule 408A of Transport Canada's Air Regulations and Aeronautics Act says in part, "No person shall act as a crew member of an aircraft while using any drug that affects his faculties to an extent that the safety of the aircraft is endangered in any way.'' The issue raised by these regulations is what dosages of what drugs are potentially dangerous. Obviously no responsible pilot uses hallucinogenics or other illegal mood-modifying drugs. Our concern here is for prescription and non-prescription drugs that allegedly relieve all of us from major and minor ailments. Medical authorities are concerned that these pills, even ones used for colds, congestion, and constipation, can be hazardous to the pilot in flight. The easiest guideline for a pilot is to avoid all drugs. If illness necessitates their use, it's possible the illness precludes flying. The pilot should consult an aeromedical officer for advice. A family physician, unfamiliar with the skills and concentration demanded by flight, may prescribe an unsafe drug. Not all responses to drugs are predictable, so the pilot must test them while he is still on the ground. Even across-the-counter drugs such as aspirin can cause an allergic reaction and sudden incapacitation. Pills taken to relieve a constant headache may delay discovery of a more serious disease.

The general result of taking many drugs is similar to consuming alcohol: the pilot's central nervous and sensory system is altered and his ability may be reduced to an unsafe level. Drugs represent a potential danger, but rate far behind alcohol as a cause of accidents in civil aviation and vehicular accidents.

Antihistamines for hay fever and other allergies can cause dizziness and also disrupt other senses, such as depth perception. They can accelerate the heart rate, cause irregular heart rhythms, raise blood pressure and, taken in large doses, can trigger a heart attack. They should not be taken within eight hours of flight. Overdoses of nasal decongestants can distort vision and physical coordination.

Drugs to combat diarrhea, especially useful for tropical countries, often are made from opium substances which cause drowsiness. Antibiotics for infections should not be taken unless the pilot decides to stay home. In any case, that's where he should be if the infection is bad. If the pilot has been anaesthetized for dental work, he should wait two days before flying. Pain-killers generally suppress mental sharpness. The long-term effects of barbiturates are not known, but when they are combined with alcohol, even in small quantities, they can cause death. Generally, pilots are advised not to take two or more drugs simultaneously because of the unpredictable, possibly violent, reactions which may occur.

Not all drugs exert a negative influence on pilot performance. Some are useful in giving relief to head and muscle pain or digestive tract discomfort and therefore uplift the pilot's disposition and skill. Cola drinks, cocoa, chocolate, tea and coffee containing stimulants can raise the level of alertness for more than an hour, depending on the amount consumed. These foods contain caffeine, a drug responsible for making some people irritable and nervous and causing irregular heart rhythm, and they can be habit forming, particularly coffee. Taken in large doses coffee causes delirium and ear-ringing and promotes the formation of peptic ulcers. People drinking six or more cups a day may be receiving a toxic dose of caffeine. Heavy coffee drinkers who try to break the habit will likely suffer withdrawal symptoms, including drowsiness and headaches. Coffee-drinking pilots "going on the wagon" should stay on the ground until severe symptoms subside. Switching to decaffeinated coffee may not totally cure the coffee-related problems of sleeplessness and stomach pains because other ingredients, such as flavouring, found in both kinds of coffee, may be the irritants. Tea can be even stronger than coffee, depending on how it's made. Cola soft drinks have about 40 per cent the amount of caffeine contained in coffee.

Caffeine is a little brother to amphetamine stimulant drugs sometimes prescribed by doctors to aid weight-loss diets. Amphetamines are also popular for their non-medical use as mood boosters, but cause sleeplessness, and impair judgment.

5. SMOKING

One addictive chemical which doesn't appear on the pilot proscribed list is nicotine. Possibly because smoking is socially accepted and the tobacco lobby so powerful, air medical administrators have closed their eyes to the effects of smoking. But several major U.S. airlines are considering a ban on passenger smoking. Aeromedical authorities should look at outlawing smoking by airborne pilots, too. Carbon monoxide in smoke restricts a smoking pilot's oxygen intake capacity and he will suffer hypoxia (the lack of sufficient oxygen) at a much lower altitude than a non-smoker. For example, a smoking pilot will experience the same effects of altitude at 10,000 feet that a non-smoking pilot will experience at 14,000 feet. A non-smoker in a closed room or cockpit with a smoker is subjected to a degree of carbon monoxide poisoning depending on the room size, smoke volume and ventilation. He may suffer a headache and general low feeling. Some individuals are allergic to smoke. The result of exposure can range from irritation to outright danger. Another source of the insidious carbon monoxide gas is a faulty heater in light aircraft.

Besides causing a slight impairment to his fitness to fly, smoking can deter a pilot from achieving a desirable level of physical fitness. Smoking increases health risks proportionate to its use. An American Cancer Society study showed that a young man smoking more than two packages of cigarettes a day will live an average of eight years less than a non-smoking man of the same age. Dr. Victoria Bradess and Dr. David Spain of New York, after conducting post-mortems on men under 50 years who died suddenly from heart attacks, noted that for every non-smoker there were sixteen who smoked more than a pack of cigarettes each day.

The immediate effect of smoke inhaled into the lungs is the reduction of physical endurance. Over a long term, smoke tar clogs the respiratory system and accelerates the resting pulse rate, lowering endurance. Carbon monoxide in smoke has a stronger attraction than oxygen to haemoglobin, so the oxygen transport capacity of blood in heavy smokers is decreased as much as 10 per cent. That translates into a significantly lower oxygen uptake capacity.

An oft-heard justification for smoking is that it maintains normal body weight, but the reasons many people gain weight in their post-smoking days may be psychological as well as physical. Smoking may have satisfied a personal craving; food replaces cigarettes. Physically, nicotine smothers taste buds. Removing the nicotine enlivens the buds and the fine taste of food is rediscovered. Eating becomes a more satisfying experience, so more is eaten. For the person kicking the habit it's best not to worry about weight increases in the first few weeks after the last cigarette. Concentrate on quitting smoking; it's a milestone, maybe the single most effective action to ensure a healthier, longer life. When pangs of temptation subside, attention can be turned to other health matters such as shedding the unwanted pounds. The liberating effect of forsaking cigarettes clears the way for the more vigorous exercises necessary to lose weight.

A good sports coach will dismiss an athlete who insists on smoking. He reasons that an athlete who is willing to risk the possibility that smoking may dull his performances has a losing attitude. The same is true in fitness: if a pilot is serious about preserving his health, he will not risk the scourge of smoking.

The more and the longer a person has smoked the tougher it is to kick the habit. Quitting is not easy, so smokers should not hesitate to seek help available from physicians, some churches, government addiction agencies and local lung and respiratory disease associations. If you're a smoking pilot who wants to quit, do it today. Not tomorrow. And when you're enduring inevitable withdrawal symptoms, remember the reward of a healthier, possibly longer life.

6. THE AUDIO-VISUAL SYSTEM

Of all the medical reasons for grounding, seeing and hearing ability have the flimsiest relation to physical fitness. They are an integral part of flying fitness, but improvements in physical fitness won't do much to alter these perception mechanisms. Eliminating certain diseases will improve seeing and hearing, and physical fitness helps overcome stress, such as fatigue, and therefore the fit pilot is more likely to interpret properly what he sees and hears; but such arguments won't help an almost blind or deaf pilot keep his licence. Nevertheless, because the audio-visual senses are an important part of flight fitness, a short discussion of them is included here.

Eyes are the most important bridge between the brain and the world. In flight, life literally depends on the pilot's vision of his instruments and the environment outside. In 1976 a coroner's jury ruled that the death of a Chicago pilot and his two passengers in a Toronto Island Airport crash was probably caused by the pilot's serious eye condition. The pilot, who was also a doctor, had had cataracts and the lenses from his eyes had been removed twenty-six years earlier. Although his glasses corrected his vision to 20-20, their thick lenses caused tunnel vision. Turning to the approach leg, he apparently lost his sense of balance, over-banked his Cessna 401 and suddenly lost altitude.

Faulty visual impressions can be traced to the eye or brain, or both. A flash of brilliant light in night darkness can stun the eye for several minutes during which images may be seen, but true vision doesn't exist. The eye may correctly perceive a scene such as a hazy horizon or fog-shrouded runway, but the mind misinterprets the image. A lack of oxygen above 6,000 feet can distort vision. Aero-sport pilots lose vision when blood is squeezed out of the optic system when performing stunts that pull with more than six to eight times the force of gravity. Other illusions are caused by vertigo (dizziness and unbalance) and autokinesis, a night-time phenomenon caused by staring too long at a single point of light. (After a while the light appears to be moving.) Aeromedical people suggest that pilots should use a scanning technique for both day and night viewing, and look to the side of what they want to see at night instead of straight at it.

It takes up to 30 minutes for the light-sensitive rods at the back of the eye to adjust to night viewing. Pilots witnessing a nearby flash of lightning at night are advised to brighten their instrument panel lighting until their eyes adjust again to true night vision. In the daytime, light is brighter at altitude because there's less atmosphere to intercept and diffuse the sun's rays. Strong light is also reflected from clouds below, so pilots should wear broad sunglasses. Smoke-grey glasses more effectively filter out harmful rays and are superior to pastel-coloured glasses. Safety is jeopardized if the pilot forgets to remove his glasses at sunset. Rain on windshields or falling on nearby land can give a false picture of what exists. Refraction of light beams through water can show the terrain lower than it actually is, a hazard to the pilot on approach. Rain can also make objects appear farther away or closer than they really are.

Fatigue, alcohol, vitamin deficiencies, drugs and even the common cold can reduce visual acuity. Smoking decreases the oxygen supply to the retina and can lower night vision as much as 25 per cent.

The eye offers doctors a first-hand view of hardened arteries and evidence of nervous disorders, anemia, high blood pressure and kidney disease. During an examination, a doctor using a tiny, bright light looks through the lens of an eye to see arteries and veins on the retinal screen. The retina is often affected by diabetes, which is sometimes responsible for the development of cataracts, one of the most common causes of blindness in North America. Special diets are often prescribed for the prevention of cataracts.

Many disturbances to vision result from aging; the lens increases in size and loses its elasticity, fluid pressure in the eye builds and causes glaucoma, and the centre of the retinal screen wears out. These conditions justify frequent eye examinations for pilots over 40. Many eye problems can be corrected with early treatment and properly fitted glasses.

Minimum standards of vision are among the most controversial in the pilot licensing regulations. For instance, the United States Federal Aviation Administration recently ruled that pilots can wear contact lenses, but contacts continue to be outlawed for commercial pilots in Canada. While these lenses offer better geometrical optics than spectacles, poorly fitted contacts can cause corneal damage and air bubbles can form between the eye and lense at high altitudes. Less contentious is the issue of colour blindness. Four per cent or more of pilot licence applicants are turned down for colour blindness, particularly for failure to distinguish red and green, which coincidentally — and unfortunately — are standard signal colours. These can't be changed because the "stop" and "go" colours are embedded in people's behaviour patterns.

The Canadian Owners and Pilots Association claims credit for convincing Transport Canada to lower colour perception requirements for pilots who were previously prohibited from night flying and also to allow some single-eyed Canadians to earn their private licences. At what point does a lower standard become a safety hazard? The answer is a common issue debated by pilots and medical officials. Captain Bob Dodds, chairman of CALPA's aeromedical committee, said that lenses required to pass pilot medicals are not suitable for flying. "Many pilots possess two sets of spectacles — one required to pass the medical and the other to fly the aircraft."

The ear is important to flight safety for two reasons: hearing and balance. Obviously a pilot must be able to hear his radio and the noise of danger such as the stall warning or the coughing of a sick engine.

The ear can be tested for its ability to detect sounds of different frequencies and intensity. Sounds are picked up by the outer ear and funnelled through a thin membrane (the eardrum) to the middle and inner ear where, by a complex system, they are converted into electrochemical impulses registering in the brain. The middle ear, a small air-filled chamber, is connected to an aperture in the back of the throat by the eustachian tube, the purpose of which is to equalize pressure on both sides of the ear drum. If the eustachian tube is clogged, as it can be when a pilot has a cold, then the middle ear is like the sealed aneroid capsule in an altimeter — it expands with altitude. If the illness is bad and the altitude too high, the eardrum can be damaged. By chewing, swallowing or yawning a healthy pilot can keep the tube open on ascents and descents. If he has a strong cold or throat infection, he should keep his feet on the ground. Connected to the inner ear is the labyrinth which contains a set of three fluid-filled canals perpendicular to each other. They provide a sense of physical balance. Motion sickness characterized by dizziness, vomiting, and random eye movements is often caused by over-stimulation of the labyrinths. Alcohol and disease, including atherosclerosis, affecting the blood circulation to the labyrinth also causes dizziness and a loss of balance.

Disorientation is common in instrument flight conditions. The horizon line is not in sight, and centrifugal force, acceleration or deceleration, may be counteracting the familiar force of gravity. Unless a pilot relies on his instruments, disorientation can be dangerous. As many as one third of all aircraft accidents are related to disorientation. While disorientation is stress enough for a healthy pilot, its effect is exaggerated on an ill pilot, particularly one with an ear infection.

Other causes of hearing loss are the ingestion of certain antibiotics, diabetes, disintegration of the bone around the middle ear, injuries, and (the most common and preventable one) exposure to noise in excess of 90 decibels. Damage depends on the length of the exposure, sound level, and the sensitivity of the individual ear. Ability to hear high-frequency sounds is the first to be damaged, and with age the impediment spreads to lower, more useful frequencies. Damaged hearing is evident in older pilots who spent their early years in louder aircraft. Although jet engines are higher pitched, their noise causes less ear damage. Jet airline pilots who complain about cockpit noise levels are likely the same ones who complain about other aviation stresses. Pilots of reciprocating engine aircraft are more justified in their complaints. The noise of a small two-or four-seat aircraft often exceeds 100 decibels on take-off, and cruise noise levels are about 90 decibels, the marginal range which can be damaging with prolonged exposure. Fortunately most private pilots don't spend enough time in the air to be concerned. But noise is a hazard for instructors, bush pilots and crop-dusters. Helicopter pilots are constantly exposed to noise in the 95 to 100 decibel range.

Those who spend long hours in noisy cockpits should obtain protective devices. Manufacturers should advise pilots what take-off and cruising decibels can be expected in each model of aircraft. Researchers are suspicious that "impulse" noises accompanying loud background noise — such as an air radio against a droning aircraft engine — are particularly damaging to ears.

7. AGING

Most airlines have a standard retirement age of 60, although there is no government law in Canada that bars a person from flying simply because he or she is getting old. But many causes of grounding are related to the aging process. Time weakens the heart, eyes, ears and makes pilots more susceptible to serious and chronic diseases. Aging retards our ability to respond quickly and efficiently and to withstand extreme weather.

It would appear, on the face of it, that nothing can be done about this all-encompassing risk factor, aging. But with a closer look, maybe there is. By launching a sound fitness program and upgrading his health habits, a pilot can slow down the aging process and hang on for a longer time to health, flying career, personal and family security, and other values and possessions in his life. Risk factors such as drinking, smoking, overeating and under-exercising can be negated with solid resolution and consistent effort. When you're 45 you don't have to look as if you are 60. You can look more like 30 or 35.

Dr. Jim Carroll of Brampton, Ontario, said that "by and large the pilots who lose their licences have a poor fitness level. There are some exceptions, but very few. A lot of pilots become blase about their futures. Especially when they become captains; some believe they've reached the pinnacle. Yet that's the time they need more motivation to stay there, to maintain themselves and their careers.''

There are more reasons than avoiding bad health and passing pilot medical examinations to justify practising daily fitness habits. For example, fitness also helps overcome stress. Pilots face unique and numerous stresses that can be more ably handled by a fit pilot. It is to those stresses that we now turn.

Pilot Stresses

Men do not usually die, they kill themselves —
Montaigne, *Essays*

Earlier we looked at the psychiatric and organic mental problems
which disqualify some pilots and licence applicants. In this chapter
we will examine external circumstances that can affect the mental
state of all pilots — diverting their attention, causing them to misin-
terpret visual and audio messages, and lowering their capacity to
make good judgments.

Stress is a force exerted upon a body that tends to strain or deform
its shape; stress on a person continued too long will cause a reaction
or compel an action. Excessive stress is distress, though both are
relative; small amounts of stress are distressing to some while large
amounts are easily handled by others.

A frequent symptom of protracted stress is the headache. Common headaches are a chemical response to fatigue or periods of high
emotion, muscular tension, anxiety, fear or frustration. Under
stress, blood pressure and blood sugar content rise while the time it
takes blood to clot decreases. Headaches are caused by an increase
in the size of sensitive blood vessels surrounding the brain. The
expansion irritates the nerves and causes pain. Most anti-headache
drugs reduce a pilot's ability to function and should not be taken
before or during flight. Continued headaches can be a symptom of
stress levels that are too high, deteriorating eyesight, or a more
serious disease. One cause of headaches is tobacco in the cockpit.

Smoke irriates eyes and sinuses, and affects night-time vision. Pilots having frequent headaches should report to their physicians. Migraine headaches can be incapacitating and are a cause for grounding.

Performance demand on a pilot is highest when he is landing an aircraft, no matter what time of day. The ability of a healthy, experienced pilot flying alone in calm weather and no air traffic obviously exceeds the demand placed on him. But a hangover, cold, fatigue or low blood sugar count may reduce his ability below demand, which has increased, perhaps, because of poor weather. The consequence of a stress-caused mental lapse can be a holocaust or an embarrassment, depending on the circumstances.

Following is a brief discussion of major stresses that can warp pilot judgment.

1. FLIGHT COMPLEXITIES

Driving an automobile requires some 12,000 human physical movements each mile, or 200 per second. That helps to explain why when speed limits were reduced during the U.S. energy shortage there was a dramatic fall in the number of fatal accidents. Given the additional stresses of G–force, noise, vibration, flicker and glare, and the extra navigational dimension of flying an aircraft, it's little wonder that psychologists ask whether modern aviation has pushed pilots beyond their capabilities. That which is new, complex or unknown, whether it's a sophisticated plane, a rental plane with unexpected idiosyncrasies, or an unfamiliar airport, increases stress. For instance, private pilots should not expect that all small airports will be less stressful than international ones. Buttonville, a light-aircraft field north of Toronto, has handled almost as many landings in recent years as each of Montreal, Vancouver and Ottawa Internationals. The sophistication of aircraft today is beyond the wildest dreams of our immediate forefathers.

Having to learn the myriad of aeronautical regulations and the performance limits of his aircraft and himself precludes a below-average intelligence person from gaining his pilot's licence. One new challenge to pilot intelligence will be the conversion to metric-numbered instruments. The ability to make numerous, rapid responses and good judgment in a complex environment can be hindered by a pilot's emotional disposition. One or a variety of problems can be upsetting emotionally: marital, family or financial difficulties, a griping crew member, the everpresent responsibility for the lives of passengers, possibly a corroded relationship between the pilots and management over working conditions and wages, or the pilot's poor physical condition and the upcoming medical.

2. FLIGHT RISKS

Risks in aviation, except for military or test pilots, are generally low, but they do exist and are a source of mental stress.

One risk has been caused by the rapid build-up of air traffic. It is expected that aircraft will carry one billion people per year by 1985 and the number will double over the following fifteen years. With too many planes and too few runways — the United States needs about four hundred more airports — congestion and the risk of mid-air collisions have increased. Risk is heightened if a pilot-in-command becomes impatient waiting in a holding pattern or to take off. Three-hour delays are not uncommon.

The most common cause of increased stress on pilots is the weather. Too often pilots underestimate weather conditions or overestimate their own and their aircraft's ability to fly in it. What makes VFR pilots dive through low clouds may forever remain a mystery because some don't survive to explain themselves. Dr. Olaf Skjenna, an aviation medical consultant, told the Canadian Owners and Pilots Association in Quebec in 1976 that many pilots chance poor weather simply to get home.

If a pilot's attitude is overly aggressive he will take unnecessary risks. The propensity to take risks changes with age, experience and responsibility. In his first few hours a student pilot is the personification of concentration and fear. Each lesson pushes him to the limits of his skill. After he has obtained his licence, he may go through the "hot pilot" stage when his actual ability is far below his personally estimated ability. He has enough hours to know how to operate his aircraft and too few to appreciate the dangers lurking in himself and the sky. Psychologists advise these pilots to guard against their own runaway egos, but that is like telling a man to jump on his own shadow. If too little fear is the bedfellow of youth, too much caution is the mate of age. Some pilots are so safety-conscious and nervous they over-correct, over-react and are therefore a danger to themselves.

3. FATIGUE

Fatigue rubs the edge off a pilot's mental and physical alertness. In its advanced state, fatigue puts the pilot to sleep. Long hours of sitting in the same environment or enduring the strain of many short flights can cause mental and physical fatigue. Just as a driver on a long road trip can become a victim of "highway hypnosis," so a pilot's environment can also have a numbing effect.

One celebrated case of fatigue was reported by the British Air Lines Pilots Association: it involved a flight to Honolulu with 125 passengers on board. The pilot was dozing at the controls. When he awoke he saw that his two co-pilots and flight engineer (the entire flight crew!) were all asleep. The Association reported that many of its pilots have fallen asleep at the controls, but this is not a practice exclusive to British pilots. Off the record, pilots in other countries, including Canada, will admit they know pilots who have fallen asleep or have done it themselves. Their stories don't surface officially because of the consequences: the guilty pilot is disciplined. In multi-member crews, the sleeper is caught in time and no harm is done. This is not to condone sleeping in the skies. Regulations against it are stringent because it weakens the safety component of any flight. For the pilot alone at the controls in a small plane, falling asleep can be fatal.

Transport Canada relates the story of a small plane with a pilot and three passengers flying at night from Winnipeg to Calgary through the northern United States. The aircraft struck the ground at cruising speed, the gear and flaps up. The aircraft bounced and flipped over, killing all inside. Evidence showed that the pilot was asleep on impact.

The pilot does not have to be asleep to demonstrate the disastrous results of advanced fatigue. Another accident report tells of three people including a pilot who were killed on a pesticide spraying mission. The burnt wreckage of the Lockheed aircraft revealed flaps were prematurely retracted on take-off. Investigators speculated that fatigue from repeated morning and evening spraying flights, combined with inhalation of the spray chemical, contributed to the pilot's apparent "deterioration of reasoning and judgment."

Transport Canada regulates against fatigue. Commerical airlines pilots and flight crew members may not spend more than 120 hours a month, or 1,200 hours a year, on flight duty unless special exemption is granted by the ministry. Flight-duty time shall not exceed 15 hours a day unless a pilot can sleep in a horizontal position in the craft while at least two other pilots are at the controls. Canadian Air Regulation 409 (2) says that a flight crew member who reaches a flight-time limitation "shall be deemed to be fatigued, and shall not continue on flight duty or be re-assigned to flight duty until such time as he has had the prescribed rest period," that being "eight consecutive hours of prone rest in the rest facility." Just to make certain that all sleepy pilots are outlawed, there's one comprehensive rule: "No person shall act as a flight crew member . . . if either the person or the [airline] operator has any reason to believe . . . that the person is suffering from or is likely to suffer fatigue, or would be otherwise unfit to properly perform his duties."

Pilots are likely the only group who have their rest time legislated. Some protest that it is unnecessary government interference; no government should have the right to tell them to go to bed. Fortunately, most airlines' contractual agreements with their pilots are considerably stricter and stipulate shorter duty hours than demanded by the law.

Enforcement of the general anti-fatigue regulations on small companies is an impossible task for government authorities in a country as vast as Canada where most remote areas depend on aviation. The myth of the adventuresome lives of bush pilots dissolves on close examination. Rather, it's a story of too many pilots chasing too few jobs, the young ones anxious to accumulate flight hours, and all pilots, young and old, working long hours for little pay. One pilot hired by bush operators in northern Canada quit because he couldn't earn enough to support his family even though he worked 16 hours a day for seven days a week during the summer. Planes and men are often abused by overuse and under-maintenance.

The British Air Lines Pilots Association has suggested that the real danger in an aircraft is "not the heart-case — the nut-case is the killer." And the Association claims that the chief contributor to mental disorders is fatigue caused by sleep disturbance. One poll of a group of U.S. professional pilots revealed that 93 per cent complained about suffering the effects of fatigue. Few get sufficient sleep prior to flights. Many put in a full day's activity or work at their second job before embarking on a night flight.

The manifestations of fatigue should be the subject of closer scrutiny in flight. The pilot himself cannot accurately assess the extent of his own fatigue. If fatigue research is to be done, some Canadian pilots say that priority should be given to the multi-stop, short-haul flights. In Great Britain daily hourly limits are reduced by 45 minutes for each leg of a flight involving several stops. One brief investigation of pilot fatigue by a Canadian television network concluded that the Canadian Air Line Pilots Association, the airline industry and the federal government should cooperate in a full-scale study of pilot fatigue. The report suggested incorporating a point system for assessing fatigue and duty limitations. Points would be awarded to each pilot within specified time periods for the number of duty hours and take-offs and landings he performs. Additional credit would be given for the time of day that flights are made, stop-over time, night flying and the crossing of time zones. When a pilot accumulates the maximum allowable "fatigue points," he is barred from flying until the time period has lapsed. The present method of deciding duty-hour maximums by contract negotiations is unsatisfactory because safety and fatigue are absolute quantities in the aviation business and should never be negotiable.

In his book *Aviation Medicine*, Dr. Kenneth Bergin defines fatigue as "a progressive decline in man's ability to carry out his appointed task, which may become apparent through deterioration in the quality of work, lack of enthusiasm, inaccuracy, lassitude, ennui, disinterestedness, a falling back in achievement or some other more indefinable symptoms." He describes three kinds of fatigue: muscular (from strenuous exercise), mental (from taxing the brain for a long time), and psychological (from emotional problems and excessive stress). The Federal Aviation Administration in the United States details two kinds of fatigue, acute and chronic. The acute or short-lived kind may be caused by lack of pre-flight sleep and rest, mild oxygen starvation, prolonged exposure to noise, uncomfortable hot or cold cockpit temperature, minor illness or aircraft vibration. Chronic or long-term fatigue may result from more serious illness, continuing emotional stress, or an uncorrected imbalance between an individual's capacity and a higher job demand. Chronic fatigue is characterized by physical weakness, insomnia, nagging tiredness, heart palpitations, depression, headaches, or a feeling of breathlessness.

Physical unfitness is the most common, albeit underrated, source of chronic fatigue. Being physically fit allows a pilot to cope better with the tension of conducting a safe and comfortable flight. Fatigue disappears suddenly when people are alarmed by an unexpected external stimulus or by a startling thought, but fatigue from boredom develops when the environment is lacking in external stimuli, or when those that are present are weak. Fighting fatigue can be done by creating jobs for yourself or conversing with members of the air crew, but the most effective stimulation is one that stirs up the circulation and forces an active response by the muscles. Moderate physical activity is the best antidote for boredom and fatigue. A few brief minutes of exercising, even without leaving your seat, can make you feel refreshed, energetic and alert.

One cause of fatigue is irregular duty hours. Ironically, sleeping when it is not required contributes to rather than eliminates fatigue. Irregular hours when accompanied by crossing time zones increases fatigue. Scientists report that humans and higher forms of life have built-in rhythms or biological clocks. Heart rate, body temperature, and other physiological phenomena such as hormone balance and haemoglobin, amino acid and blood sugar levels are subject to a daily pattern. Basal heart rate can vary up to 25 per cent between sleeping and waking hours and temperatures are almost one degree Celsius lower during sleep. Whether we are "day" or "night" people, our reaction times and intellectual and conceptual capacities change hourly according to a constant pattern each 24-hour period. In his paper, "Diurnal Variations," Edgar Folk, Jr. wrote that a person's "reaction to drugs is different at noon and at midnight; the accuracy and the speed with which arithmetical problems are solved differ by the hour; in industry, subjects who have not converted their status to that of being night workers when they were formerly day workers cause more accidents and make more errors in tending machines or reading indicator boards. These errors are most likely to happen at 3 a.m. There have been few studies, if any, of the success in physical performance when participants are asked to perform at unusual times.''

Daily rhythms cannot be readjusted as fast as jets can cross time zones. One rule of thumb is that it takes one day to change the circadian cycle by one hour. Therefore if a person has moved across six time zones, it would take him six days to adjust. This fatigue phenomenom, sometimes described as jet lag, is an inconvenience for occasional travellers, a worry for coaches of sports teams, and of concern to many pilots who experience its effects on a daily basis.

Some pilots discount the effects of daily rhythm adjustment. A pilot may feel fatigue, but from other causes. He may be flying to faraway exotic cities full of pleasures and possibly a mistress. Sleep is forsaken as he succumbs to the temptations and adventures. Or maybe he took off from New York in the evening, flew through the night and landed at Paris, Rome or Athens in the morning. His body demands sleep. His eyes, squinting at the sunlight, tell him the day is just beginning. He will have difficulty sleeping eight hours in the different environment. The quality of his sleep will be adversely affected by the hardness, or softness, of his mattress, room temperature and relative humidity and noise from other rooms and hallways of his hotel or the street outside. And sunlight filtering through the windows can't be totally blocked out.

There's little question that circadian rhythms exist and, when altered, exert at least a subtle stress on people who cross time zones. Persons travelling west usually are influenced less than those travelling east because westward bound people can begin immediately on a new sleep cycle and that accelerates the change to a new rhythm. Many pilots prefer to travel westward on round-the-world flights because it's less tiring for them to let local time catch up when they have landed. Airlines have considered the possibility of introducing ''time zone'' or ''time lock'' hotels for pilots which would allow them to eat, sleep and otherwise live on the same time clock as their hometown.

Some corporations send their executives overseas one or two

days early so that they will be totally alert and more effective for business meetings. Athletes and business people can reduce the effects of altered circadian rhythms by preparing for several days in advance of a flight by going to bed progressively earlier or later to adjust to the clock of their destination. A minimum-rest-period calculator is available for world travellers which suggests the minimum number of hours a traveller should rest between flights. Pilots aren't permitted such a luxury, although the bid system which allows each pilot some choice of when and where he will fly helps him suit the workload to his personal needs and tolerances.

Fatigue, and indeed other forms of stress, affects each pilot differently. A pilot on the lookout for stress may convince himself that he is more tired than he really is. Others more relaxed about their work are sometimes oblivious to external pressures. Too much sensitivity to fatigue raises anxiety and prematurely brings on objective fatigue, and too little can cause a pilot to fly fatigued when his performance has dipped below a safe level. A pilot can justifiably blame duty schedules, the tension of responsibility, circadian rhythms, high altitudes, or a host of other possibile causes of fatigue; but first he should look to causes he can eliminate, and fortify himself against fatigue stresses by improving his physical fitness.

4. ALTITUDE FLYING

Flying, unpresssurized, at high altitudes heightens fatigue. Physical fitness and freedom from the smoking habit, anemia and other maladies will improve a pilot's tolerance of high altitudes. Although airline pilots, except in some emergencies, are protected from the cold, and from low oxygen and atmospheric pressures of high altitude flying, these conditions are encountered by private pilots. At 5 kilometres high the temperature is 40 degrees Celsius colder, and oxygen and air pressure are half their sea-level value. The pressure that oxygen in the air exerts on the blood, so that it can perform its life-sustaining business, determines to a large extent the volume carried in the circulation system. As the human body is elevated above the earth's surface, the ratio of oxygen to carbon dioxide and water vapour in the lungs undergoes a progressive change, from a higher to lower percentage of oxygen and a lower to higher percentage of carbon dioxide and water vapour. At 3¹/₂ kilometres high, a pilot begins to lose some manual dexterity. At 4 to 5 kilometres the mental and physical handicaps become worse. He feels sleepy and may have a slight headache. His lips and fingernails have a bluish hue and his vision begins to dim. His judgment is impaired and behaviour modified. At 5 kilometres and higher normal pilot abilities quickly become non-existent. At 6¹/₂ kilometres convulsions may be experienced and unconsciousness is a certainty.

To appreciate the devastating effects of altitude, consider that if cabin compression is lost at 30,000 feet up, a pilot could lose consciousness within 15 seconds. A good reason to be familiar with oxygen equipment.

Oxygen starvation is termed hypoxia. The sinister aspect of hypoxia is that its victim may not recognize he is being affected. Lack of oxygen blurs a pilot's judgment, particularly to his own shortcomings. He shows the familiar signs of intoxication — a slowness of movement and an abandon of physical coordination.

In some ways, the effects on the circulation system from high altitude flying are similar to anaerobic exercise — in other words, there is a build-up of lactic acid in the muscles. Light exercise, including getting out of the seat and moving around periodically during the flight, will stimulate the body to take in more oxygen and remove the lactic acid. Regular drinks of juice or water, not tea or coffee, will help combat low humidity levels. Blinking sponges the eyeballs, relieving the dryness of the eyes caused by low humidity.

The U.S. Federal Aviation Administration recommends that no pilot should fly above 15,000 feet without pressurization or oxygen equipment. Prolonged flights at much lower altitudes can produce hypoxia and headaches. Oxygen is necessary to maintain good vision in darkness so it should be carried by pilots flying more than a mile high at night.

Even a small loss of blood through personal injury or a donation to the Red Cross precludes flying at high altitudes for one or two days. High altitudes and associated stresses can trigger rapid breathing and heart rates. Involuntary hyperventilation is a warning, and the pilot should take measures immediately to correct the problem. If it persists, he should talk to his co-pilot, or if alone, talk to himself.

The slower cadence of conversation will help him return to a normal breathing rate. Breathing into a paper bag or cupped hands are also quick cures.

The low pressure of high altitude forces gases trapped in the ear, sinuses and stomach to try to escape. Pilots should throw convention to the wind, as it were, and belch and fart when the urge presents itself. The condition can also be relieved by slowing down the vertical air speed. If gases aren't expelled, pressure in the body causes bloating, discomfort, even pain. Because intestinal gases result from swallowing air along with food, the problem can be avoided by refusing large meals before the flight, and carbonated beverages, gaseous foods and chewing gum during the flight. Again, the benefits of good physical fitness cannot be underestimated; fitness improves the digestive function.

A pilot with nasal or throat congestion, or a common cold should avoid flying in an aircraft that doesn't have a pressurized cabin. After suffering a minor head or chest illness, the pilot can check whether he's ready to fly by performing a simple test: squeeze the nostrils together to prevent the passage of air. Swallow twice. If the ears feel like ballons being blown up, the eustachian tubes are clear and the ears won't be a source of pain at altitude. To release the air in the ears, swallow again without clamping the nose shut.

5. BACKACHES

Severe back pain, particularly in the lower regions, is the second most common reason, next to the ordinary cold, for the temporary grounding of pilots. One out of every two professional pilots will be absent a considerable number of work hours in his career because of a debilitating back pain. While backaches are a scourge for the general population, pilots are especially vulnerable because they are seated and motionless for most of their working hours.

The shock-absorbing cushions between vertebrae lose much of their moisture and grow brittle with age. The aging process is accelerated by poor posture, obesity, and the absence of good muscles in the back and abdominal area. A heavy stomach drags the spinal column forward, increasing its curvature and placing uneven stress on the intervertebral pads. In advanced conditions of lumbar lordosis, nerves are pinched and sharp pains may be felt in the legs.

The greatest pressure on the spine is normally exerted when a body is seated, not standing or walking. People usually relax their abdominal muscles more when they're seated, and many kinds of chairs do not offer proper support to the spine. The seat (horizontal) portion should be flat or tilted slightly forward and be at a height to allow the top of the thighs to be parallel to the floor when the feet are flat on the floor. The back of the chair should be straight or firm or possibly curved to the natural slight inward (toward the stomach) contour of the lower spine. The backs of many "easy," swivel, bus and airplane passenger chairs are curved the wrong way.

Some pilot seats are uncomfortable and not conducive to maintaining good posture. A recent survey by the International Federation of Air Line Pilots Association revealed that 36 per cent of more than 1,300 pilots, flight engineers and navigators suffered frequent and severe backaches. Most of those surveyed were working in Boeing 707s and 747s. Only 18 per cent never had backaches. Ninety-five per cent of the complainers said their backaches were caused by cockpit conditions, but no particular seat design was singled out as the offender. More than one kind of seat is installed in each aircraft type. A vast variety of seats are in use in commercial aircraft. Airline companies must be encouraged to search for seats designed for good posture. Pilot seats should have adjustable back and lumbar support, ventilated seat coverings and comfortable upholstery material.

Besides the threat that backache may temporarily or permanently ground a pilot, there is no doubt it impairs pilot performance and is sometimes accompanied by other illnesses in the stomach, urinary tract and intestines. Aviation researchers note that backache is one pathological stress that makes the suffering pilot three times more accident prone than one in a healthy condition.

Back pains appear and reappear, often at unpredictable intervals, and the frequency usually increases until the pilot is driven to do something about it. Pain is caused by overstressing the moving parts of the spine. As one grows older the tolerance to stress wanes and more time is needed between stressful periods for recovery. If the pilot fails to take corrective action, the condition causing the backache may become so severe that the value of a therapeutic exercise and posture program is nullified. An operation may be necessary, such as the removal of the damaged disc or discs, a widening of a channel to ease the pressure on the pinched spinal nerve, or an enzyme injection into the disc to dissolve the portion causing the painful friction.

Military history has taught us to appreciate bad posture. Standing stiffly at attention accentuates the inward curve of the lower spine and generally causes unnecessary tension down the spine. Stress should be removed by straightening the spine and relaxing the muscles, tendons and ligaments surrounding it. Methods of restoring and maintaining good posture by performing regular back and abdominal exercises are outlined in a later chapter.

6. OVERCOMING STRESS

Stress puts lines in our faces and turns our hair prematurely grey. Although not so obvious nor as damaging to our vanity, the same wear and tear is occurring on our vital organs and body tissue. Pilots face the insidious stress of immobility. Some spend 14 to 16 hours a day just sitting down.

But all people under stress undergo the same biological responses as prehistoric man and our recent ancestors. Adrenalin flows, heart rate increases, blood pressure rises, digestive processes slow down, and we are keyed for action. But we no longer live in a fight or flight world. We can't run from the cockpit or punch the first officer. If stress is increased, our muscles become taut and burn energy, and the blood vessels constrict. While all kinds of solutions to combatting unrelieved stress are proposed, none is more effective than planned exercise. About $500 million is spent each year in the United States on tranquillizers and sleeping pills. A fitness program is cheaper and has better effect. Exercise consumes ingredients in the body created by stress. It stretches and loosens tight muscles and offers temporary relief from mental problems. Exercise returns the body and mind to a normal state, making it easier later to socialize, work and sleep.

Kingsley Ward, a private Canadian pilot who survived open-heart surgery to fly again, wrote about the solution to stress in *Canadian*

Flight magazine in 1976: "Go fishing a little more often — not to catch fish so much as to enjoy a little solitude and a change of pace. You won't have to worry about losing your [pilot's] licence for medical reasons if you simply make it a habit to look after yourself as well as you probably look after your airplane. . . . The body is somewhat like an aircraft engine. It performs better with use rather than standing in the hangar."

One other means of reducing stress is to avoid it. Much stress is self-imposed. People don't know when enough is enough. They heap burden upon burden, never saying no, never spending sufficient time on any one project or personal relationship. Sleep, diet, physical and mental rest are neglected. Doing too much, they grow tense, nervous and, in severe situations, suffer hypertension and mental depression. One result of tension is the involuntary tightening of muscles throughout the body. Relaxing is easier said than done. Much tension is unconscious, uncontrollable. Trying to "think ourselves down" fails when we don't know the techniques. Thinking too much is often the original problem. Like insomnia, we can't just think ourselves to sleep or into a state of relaxation. A rested mind is one in which doubts and concerns aren't flashing around.

Techniques such as meditation and hypnotism are often bathed in an aura of mysticism and based on the fact that if a person concentrates on a single idea, word or object, his mind can relax, and through it, the body. A technique using electronic gadgetry in vogue in recent years is biofeedback. By employing trial and error and concentration some biofeedback patients claim they can exert control over their intestines, liver, heart, brain and kidneys. Electronic monitoring of pulse beat, brain waves, blood pressure, body temperature and muscle tension aids in regulating what were previously regarded as involuntary body processes. Besides claiming that the effects of stress are reduced and headaches banished, some advocates of biofeedback believe it can cure a variety of diseases, including hypertension and heart disease. While it would be unfair to dismiss such serious attempts to find meaningful ways to reduce stress, a simpler solution is regular exercise.

5 *Fitness Can Keep You Flying*

It's better to relieve flight stress with a little sweat than a large martini.

North American society is preoccupied with disease and stress — simply because we have so much of it. Hospital expansions can't keep up to the demands of sickness. Patients wait months, sometimes years, to see medical specialists or for a hospital bed for non-emergency surgery. Medical costs are astronomical. The alarming disease statistics tell only a part of the story: behind each statistic is a personal tale of suffering, days or months of unemployment, unfulfilment and unhappiness, bedsores, ashen complexions, fear and bitterness. Engrossed in this national problem, we overlook the cause.

The human body adapts to habitual demands. One of the significant changes to human life in the twentieth century has been the reduction in the need for exertion. In earlier years, people chopped wood, pumped water, shovelled coal, and scrubbed clothes on a washboard. Today there's an electrical device for almost every chore. People can get through a day without doing more than walking to the dinner table and brushing their teeth, unless they have an electric toothbrush! The average businessman spends 14 to 16 waking hours sitting down. Little wonder that a few years ago, when Yankee Stadium was rebuilt, seats had to be widened from the original 19 to 23 inches. Without activity, muscles lose strength, physical reserves dry up, and the circulatory system and reflexes slow down. Hippocrates said, "That which is used, grows; that which is not used, withers."

Some aeromedical and pilot leaders in Canada are discouraged by the apathetic attitude of most pilots toward fitness. Captain Harvey Bergen of Toronto, local aeromedical chairman for CALPA's Air Canada pilots, estimated that 20 per cent of pilots don't care about fitness. Sixty per cent do care but do nothing about it. The remaining 20 per cent are doing something, but probably not enough. Bergen suggested that "Air Canada should give each pilot $100 a year to join a fitness club. It would be the best investment the company could make. Pilots of course would have to show evidence of membership and participation."

A medical questionnaire of 464 CALPA pilots in 1973 revealed that 65 per cent of young pilots made little or no effort to engage in regular exercise routines. Most said they were bored with exercises or didn't have time to do them. Among those who claimed to exercise regularly were some who considered playing golf or making any voluntary muscle movement a fitness-building exercise! Ten per cent of the younger pilots owned exercise bicycles compared to 50 per cent of older pilots.

Obviously everyone wants good health and a long life. Unfortunately, the choice is not really available. We are only given a "chance" to live well and long, and we can improve that "chance" by reducing health risk factors. We stack the odds against ourselves by believing that fate or medicine will save us. We are sometimes falsely insulated against a full appreciation of the tragedy that befalls those who lose their gamble; we think that statistics and bad news are for the other guy. Marked by the production of drugs for almost every ailment, immunizations for smallpox, polio and diphtheria, and surgical marvels such as heart and lung transplants, medicine over the past half-century is challenging religion as a saviour of men. Some doctors themselves say that such blind respect for medicine is not healthy. People can rely too much on their doctors and ignore the first source of defence against illness — themselves! During the past seventy years there has been a dramatic change in the leading causes of death in North American populations — from infectious to "behavioural" diseases. More people are dying from causes that they've helped bring on themselves. For instance, in Canada in 1974, of those who died at ages earlier than predicted averages, accidents and suicides accounted for 37 per cent, and heart disease and respiratory disease (primarily lung cancer) 23 per cent.

Recognizing that behavioural changes can improve health and cut costs (health care in Canada is $500 per capita per year, $600 in the United States), the Canadian government has established two major goals, described by former Health and Welfare Minister Marc Lalonde: ". . . improvement of the social and physical environment, and modification of certain living habits that influence the level of health and fitness." But the government is aware of the difficulties in promoting an alteration in behaviour, especially when it calls for personal sacrifice such as cutting back on a heavy diet, drinking and smoking, and becoming more physically active. Despite apprehensions, the government launched its "Operation Lifestyle" plan in the 1970s and bombarded the Canadian public with a number of programs to heighten the awareness of individual health and fitness (mostly, the lack of that fitness) and ways to improve it.

The "Health Hazard Appraisal," available free through some local health authorities, offers individuals a deeper insight into their own lifestyles and, with the aid of a computer in Ottawa, gives advice on how to improve their chances of living a longer, healthier life. The government also started Participaction, a successful nonprofit, private company that has been prodding Canadians (via television, radio and newspaper ads) to get off their sitdown lawn mowers and run around the block. Participaction went further than some government officials might have hoped. The company marketed fitness by doing such things as rewriting the national anthem: "We stand on guard for thee / The true north soft and free." And the messages weren't flattering: it said that most Canadians are overweight, out of shape and many are cardiac candidates. It noted that bridge is our most popular game, and to reduce the effort of playing, participants can put their cards in automatic shufflers. Participaction charged that too often Canadian school gymnasiums are shut down because janitors are worried that kids will leave scuff marks on polished floors.

Airline pilots associations share this enthusiasm for disease prevention through fitness. Officials of the Air Line Pilots Association in the United States have recommended setting up a task force to consider "a workable program that would establish prevention as the core of an approach to the health problems of airline pilots. We believe that prevention should be the primary motivating factor of medical effort within the industry and the F.A.A." In the United

States some 40 per cent of health care funding is spent on hospitalization and only 3 per cent on disease prevention and control. Less than .05 per cent is for health education.

While no absolute proof can be offered to show that raising fitness levels through exercise leads to a reduction in heart and some other diseases, there is little question that daily exercise can reduce the impact of known risk factors such as hypertension and obesity. And both evidence and intuition is overwhelmingly in favour of the supposition that the lack of fitness is itself a risk factor.

Too often our actions are influenced by social norms and pressures and not by necessity. Some countries are more enlightened than Canada about the life-saving value of exercise. Adults jogging on Canadian streets in full public view are more often ridiculed than applauded. Rather than face the harsh music, some fitness candidates fall expediently into the abyss of unhealth already occupied by their hecklers. Older people appear more sensitive to the opinions of ill-informed neighbours and bystanders. The irony is that older people are usually more in need of fitness training. Unattended bodies tend to atrophy.

Pilot fitness is the long-term capacity and ability to perform routine duties with a minimum of fatigue and discomfort and to be physically and mentally alert to meet and overcome the toughest challenges aviation has to offer. This degree of fitness offers a bonus dividend: it equips the pilot to live more enjoyably in off-duty hours. Taking care of the body helps one's mental disposition, although it is difficult to measure these benefits objectively. But physiological well-being, such as muscular strength, tone and flexibility, can be measured. While such external fitness gains much attention from our society (which dwells on appearances), it is not as crucial as internal fitness. Survival is possible without strong muscles but not without a functioning heart. In absolute fitness terms, the average body-builder or weightlifter doesn't measure up to a skinny, well-trained jogger. There's no clear separation of internal and external fitness. A good posture and muscle-skeletal structure assist the function of the internal organs and blood circulatory system. While it's possible to build the external body to the detriment of the internal body — witness super heavy-weight weight lifters — the reverse is impossible. Ideal fitness includes the highest possible cardio-respiratory strength and efficiency. In pursuing that ideal, some, but possibly not all, necessary external fitness will be achieved.

Routine endurance exercises practised by previously sedentary persons lower their resting pulse rate and increase the blood stroke volume of the heart during the exercise and at rest. One measure of cardio-respiratory fitness is the ability to take in oxygen (to the lungs), distribute it (through the circulation system) and utilize it (in the muscles) to release energy. When body weight and pulse rate from a measured workload are taken into account, maximum oxygen uptake capacity can be calculated. This oxygen utility score — the most important single measure of fitness — declines measurably during adult years. It is enormously responsive to regular physical training in which rapid heart rates are achieved. A fit 60-year-old can have a higher oxygen uptake capacity than an average 25 or 30-year old. A high level of fitness also means the heart rate will return to its resting level sooner than that of a sedentary person who has completed the same volume of work.

Standards of fitness and good health are related to what and how much a person eats, where he lives (city or country, rich or poor nation), whether he lives alone or with family or relatives, his economic position, race, and age, and who his parents are. The American Medical Association says the healthiest American is a young farm boy in the north central part of the United States who has reasonably healthy parents. While a person is condemned or blessed to live in the body he was born in, he must take heart that even some of the worst genetic disasters have been overcome by thoughtful planning and diligent work. Inspiration and continuing motivation is needed to make a significant improvement in a person's fitness lifestyle.

A point that is overwhelmingly simple — the best planned fitness program is useful only to persons who perform it! Talking or reading about a program may have some small social or academic benefits but its best value is as an encouragement and guide to pilots who will actually carry it out. Unfortunately, too many fitness programs are used as cures and not preventive measures. Some of the most dedicated converts to fitness are cardiac patients or persons with serious maladies who discover almost too late the value of fit living. Brushing elbows with death is a great motivator, but so many die trying. Or not trying!

Getting a Certificate of Body Worthiness

Fitness can help you make both ends meet.

Fitness has no pied piper luring the sedentary pilot into a new lifestyle. The truths about fitness are simple and self-evident to its practitioners, who have made a personal commitment to become physically fit. It would be misleading to promote fitness as the cure of all illnesses and stresses. Life and flying aren't that uncomplicated.

Maybe you have made sporadic efforts to get fit. Maybe you bought an exercise bicycle or weight-training set that is stashed in a downstairs cupboard. We hope we've convinced you to begin again, this time armed with a firm commitment and a sound program. The first step is to discover your level of fitness.

1. PRE-ASSESSMENT

Before assessing your fitness, make certain that you can withstand moderate physical stress without endangering your health. Have a medical examination, particularly if you're over 35. Tell the doctor of your intentions to begin a program of physical activity. Most pre-exercise program pilots won't need a medical, but you will want a doctor to tell you that! It would be unwise not to have a medical if you have had heart trouble, chest pains, dizzy spells, hypertension, arthritis or other serious medical problems. Or if you have been living a sedentary life. There is no universally accepted medical examination procedure for giving a person a certificate of body worthiness. Doctors must judge whether you're ready for the stress of a fitness assessment. Your medical should include a stress test so your electrocardiogram can be studied while your heart is beating faster than its resting rate. Heart irregularities sometimes don't show up at rest but are apparent at a higher rate.

When you've been cleared by the doctor, you should rate your performance capacity. How fit are you? Your fitness assessment will help you decide what specifics should be built into your exercise program. Following are descriptions of methods of assessing your fitness — from a single self-assessment heart performance test (which has high possibility of error), to the more comprehensive Advanced Fitness Assessment (slightly lower possibility of error), and finally, to the sophisticated tests by fitness experts (recommended for their accuracy), which are explained in detail after these tests.

SELF-ASSESSMENT

Give your body a walk around. Use the same objectivity and scrutiny that you use to check your own aircraft.

First, look at your naked self in a full-length mirror. Inspect the front, sides, and back. Look for bulky areas. Are your cheeks heavy? Is that a double, or a triple chin? Is there slippage here or there, a roll around your middle? Has your navel squished flat in fat? Has your rear end sagged? Is there so much fat on your thighs that ripples have formed and they jiggle when you move? Now, see if you can find a photograph of yourself when you were in your early twenties. Sure, some of the changes have happened just because you're older now. But how much of the difference is because you've let yourself go? The degree to which you've allowed that to happen is the degree you're out of shape.

Try the pinch test. With your thumb and index finger, pinch up the skin and underlying fat on your abdomen at your beltline, then your

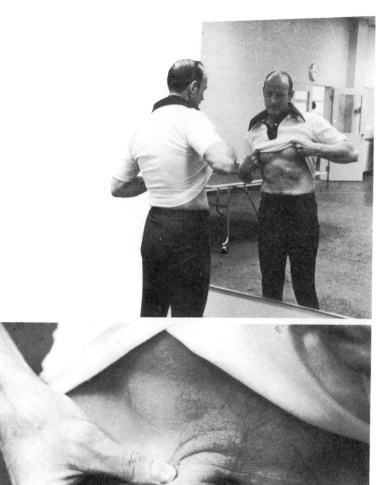

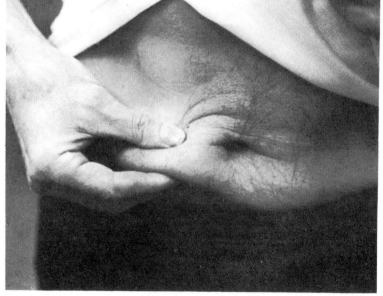

waist near your kidneys, your upper chest near your shoulder, the back of your upper arm and the front of your thigh. If the skinfold thickness that you are able to pinch up in any of these areas is more than $1/2$ inch (13 millimetres) you have excess fat. If the thickness is as much as 1 inch (25 millimetres) your fitness program should include dieting. Don't be misled by a standard height-weight chart. It provides only a general guide and doesn't take into account an individual's portions of bone, muscle and fat. It's possible to be "overweight" but not overly fat, and "underweight" and carry too much fat.

Next, discover your resting pulse rate. You can easily count your own pulse rate by placing three fingers of one hand on the thumbside of the wrist on your other hand. Another pulse can be found on either side of your Adam's apple under the back of the jaw bone. Take the pulse on only one side of your neck. Don't press hard. Exercise, eating, some drugs and coffee, emotional disruption and warm temperatures will raise pulse rates. Even the anxiety of reading your own pulse can increase it a few beats per minutes. Try to get the lowest reading. It may be obtained in the morning before getting out of bed, although some people can achieve even lower rates by performing extremely mild exercise and then resting a few minutes.

A range from 60 to 100 beats per minute can be considered normal for the resting heart, although a rate in the 70s is most common. In the normally healthy person, a low resting heart rate is preferable to one that is high, and is usually consistent with a good level of physical fitness. Well-conditioned endurance athletes have been known to have resting heart rates in the 30s and 40s.

One common cause of a high rate is obesity and lack of fitness. The heart is straining just to keep the big body idling. Because pulse rates are closely aligned to oxygen consumption, they are a fairly good measure of fitness. Given a certain workload, such as jogging or running upstairs, the lower the heart rate, the better the fitness. However, like most instant indicators of fitness, be shy of accepting pulse rates as an absolute. Great individual differences have been recorded without any obvious explanation.

Heart Performance Test

Here is a simple basic test of your heart's performance. It should be done quietly in a cool room. You will need a watch with a second hand and a sturdy box, chair or step, exactly 16 inches (40 centimetres) high. You may have some difficulty getting an accurate score the first time. If so, try it again a day or two later. *(Note: If you choose to do the more comprehensive pilots' advanced fitness assessment on the following pages, it is not necessary to do this heart performance test.)*

Step One

Lie on your back on the floor, arms resting at your sides. Breathe slowly and deeply. Relax. After five minutes, slowly move your hand to your neck and count your pulse for 15 seconds. Multiply by four to find your heart rate for one minute.

Step Two

Now stand up slowly, wait 10 seconds and then count your pulse again. The difference between the lying and standing pulse rates tells a story. Gravity exerts a standard predictable force on a column of blood in a body suddenly altered from a horizontal to vertical position. Some people will show no difference at all. Zero to 12 beats difference is good and 12 to 16 average. If you're over 16 beats your heart-circulatory system is not as efficient as it should be.

Step Three

Do this modified step test. Using the sturdy box, step, or chair exactly 16 inches high, step up fully and down for one minute at a rate of 30 step-ups per minute. Immediately check your pulse rate, then sit down and rest comfortably for one minute before counting it once more. Total your lying, standing, after exercise, and recovery pulse rates and see where your total is on this table:

TOTAL	RATING
Up to 300	Excellent
301 — 320	Very Good
321 — 340	Good
341 — 370	Fair
371 — 390	Moderately Low
391 — 410	Low
over 410	Very Low

For example, if you have a resting pulse of 72, standing pulse of 76, (immediate) after exercise pulse of 104, and recovery (after one minute) pulse of 80, you would have a total of 332 or Good. Because factors such as age, weight, and emotions affect your heart rate the preceding test is only a crude indication of your fitness.

ADVANCED FITNESS ASSESSMENT TEST FOR PILOTS

A more detailed series of five tests are presented on the following pages. On the final page there's a Personal Fitness Profile. The sum of your scores gives you a more accurate, but certainly not perfect, assessment of your fitness level. Completing these tests will require time and effort. If you plan to have your fitness assessed by experts, you may wish to skip this series, although it would be of interest to compare your own to a professional assessment of your fitness. Keep in mind that these are rudimentary tests. They are fun to do and may give you a rough estimate of where you are on the fitness ladder. For the most valid results, read the instructions carefully and perform the tests exactly as described:

1. Take the test when you are feeling rested and relaxed. If you are rushed, or not feeling well, the results will be misleading.
2. Do not smoke, eat or drink coffee or an alcoholic beverage, or participate in vigorous physical activity during the two hours preceding the test.
3. Gather together the items you require before starting the test: pencil, paper, 12 inch (30 centimetre) stepping box, or available stair, clock or watch with second hand, body-weight scales, tape measure at least 48 inches (120 centimetres), 3 ft. (1 metre) ruler.
4. Wear light, comfortable clothing and take the test in a comfortable environment at approximately 20 degrees Celsius.
5. Lie down quietly for five minutes before starting the test.
6. Take the tests only in the sequence indicated.
7. If at any point during the tests you experience pain, extreme fatigue, dizziness or any unusual discomfort, stop immediately. Before you try again, have a recheck from your doctor.
8. If you take the test for a second or third time to measure your progress, do it at the same time of day under conditions similar to your first test.

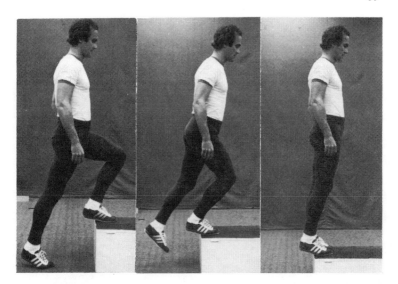

Three-Minute Step Test:

This simple test offers an approximate measure of your cardio-respiratory fitness. Find a sturdy step-up box, chair or stool 12 inches high and a stop-watch or a watch with a sweep second hand. Wear light, comfortable shoes without a raised heel, or wear no shoes at all.

- Standing with feet together, facing the step, start your watch, and step up with the right foot, then with the left, then step down with the right followed by the left in a 4-count cadence. Continue for three minutes at a pace of 30 complete step-ups per minute. Thirty seconds after beginning you should be completing your fifteenth step-up. If your pace is slow or fast, make an appropriate adjustment, so that at 60 seconds you are completing your 30th step-up. Continue to monitor your pace. *Note:* It is important to equalize leg work by changing the lead leg every 30 seconds. When finished the three minutes immediately sit down and take your pulse for 10 seconds, multiply the figure by six and record your per minute rate. Walk around for a minute or two until you are feeling fully recovered.

60

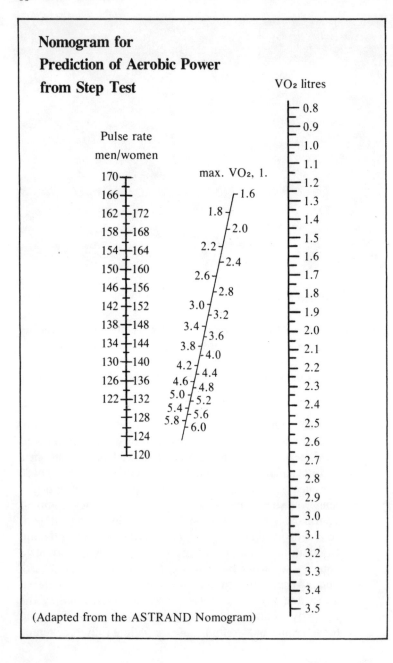

Nomogram for
Prediction of Aerobic Power
from Step Test

VO₂ litres

Pulse rate
men/women

(Adapted from the ASTRAND Nomogram)

How to Score Your Cardio-Respiratory Fitness (based on the 3-minute step test):

A few simple mathematical computations are necessary to calculate your predicted maximum oxygen uptake, or aerobic power.

1. Convert your body weight from pounds to kilograms by dividing by 2.2 (i.e., a 220 pound man weighs 100 kg).
2. Multiply .3048 x your body weight (in kg) x 30 to determine your workload.
3. Your oxygen uptake (VO_2) equals (0.003 × your workload) + 0.30 (for men), (0.003 x your workload) + 0.25 (for women)
4. On the accompanying nomogram draw a straight line from the VO_2 figure on the right-hand scale (as calculated in 3 above) to your post-exercise heart rate (after your 3-minute step test) on the left-hand scale.
5. The point where the line you have drawn crosses the middle scale is your predicted maximum oxygen uptake, but it must be corrected for your age by multiplying it by the following "correction factor."

Closest Age		Correction Factor
25	—	1.00
35	—	0.87
45	—	0.78
55	—	0.71
65	—	0.65

6. Convert the resulting figure (your predicted oxygen uptake corrected for age, expressed in litres of oxygen per minute) to millilitres per kilogram body weight per minute by multiplying by 1000 and then dividing that figure by your body weight in kilograms.
7. The resulting figure is your predicted maximum oxygen uptake expressed in millilitres of oxygen per kilogram of body weight per minute (ml/kg/min). In the accompanying chart find your uptake rating and corresponding point value.

The figures in the following two charts have been obtained from data gathered from over 2700 tests carried out on members at the Fitness Institute. The figures and resulting fitness standards, therefore, have been derived from individuals of above average fitness.

MEN

20-29	30-39	40-49	50-59	60-69	Rating	Points
65.1+	59.5+	54.9+	51.9+	49.8+	*Excellent*	50
59.0 – 65.1	53.4 – 59.5	48.8 – 54.9	45.8 – 51.9	43.7 – 49.8	*Very Good*	42
52.8 – 59.0	47.2 – 53.4	42.6 – 48.8	39.6 – 45.8	37.5 – 43.7	*Good*	35
46.7 – 52.8	41.1 – 47.2	36.5 – 42.6	33.5 – 39.6	31.4 – 37.5	*Fair*	28
40.6 – 46.7	35.0 – 41.1	30.4 – 36.5	27.4 – 33.5	25.3 – 31.4	*Moderately Low*	21
34.5 – 40.6	28.9 – 35.0	24.3 – 30.4	21.3 – 27.4	19.2 – 25.3	*Low*	14
34.4 or less	28.8 or less	24.2 or less	21.2 or less	19.1 or less	*Very Low*	7

WOMEN

20-29	30-39	40-49	50-59	60-69	Rating	Points
60.8 +	56.1 +	53.7+	51.2 +	47.7 +	*Excellent*	50
54.2 – 60.8	49.5 – 56.1	47.1 – 53.7	44.5 – 51.2	41.1 – 47.7	*Very Good*	42
47.5 – 54.2	42.8 – 49.5	40.4 – 47.1	37.9 – 44.5	34.4 – 41.1	*Good*	35
40.8 – 47.5	36.1 – 42.8	33.7 – 40.4	31.2 – 37.9	27.7 – 34.4	*Fair*	28
34.2 – 40.8	29.5 – 36.1	27.1 – 33.7	24.6 – 31.2	21.1 – 27.7	*Moderately Low*	21
27.5 – 34.2	22.8 – 29.5	20.4 – 27.1	17.9 – 24.6	14.4 – 21.1	*Low*	14
27.4 or less	22.7 or less	20.3 or less	17.8 or less	14.3 or less	*Very Low*	7

2. Percentage of Body Fat Calculation

For home use, the following procedure can be used to estimate your percentage of body fat. This system was developed by exercise physiologists J. H. Wilmore and A. R. Behnke and is only accurate when used with men. Female readers should give themselves an "estimated" rating based on our previously described "pinch" test.

For male readers, first weigh yourself without clothing. Second, take your waist measurement (at navel level) to the closest half-inch. The tape should be snug but not depress the skin. Stand relaxed to obtain a true measurement. Holding your stomach in will give a false reading. To estimate your body fat percentage:

1. Multiply your body weight in pounds by 1.082.
2. From the resulting figure subtract 4.15 × your waist measurement in inches.
3. To the resulting figure, add 98.42. (This figure represents your *lean body weight*.)
4. Subtract your **lean body weight** from your true body weight.
5. Multiply the resulting figure by 100.
6. Divide that figure by your body weight.

The result is your body fat expressed as a percentage of your total body weight.

MEN			WOMEN	
% Body Fat	Points	Rating	Pinch Test	Points
less than 10.0	20	*Excellent*	1/2″	20
10.1 - 12.5	16	*Very Good*	3/4″	16
12.6 - 15.1	13	*Good*	1″	13
15.2 - 18.2	10	*Fair*	1 1/4″	10
18.3 - 21.2	6	*Moderately Low*	1 1/2″	6
21.3 - 24.0	3	*Low*	1 3/4″	3
24.1 +	0	*Very Low*	2″	0

64

3. 30-Second Sit-Up Test

Strength of the abdominal muscles is an important factor. Eighty per cent of low back problems can be attributed to weakness in low back and abdominal muscles. Ideally, your relaxed waist measurement should be six inches less than your normal chest measurement. One insurance company concluded from a study of policy-holders that for every inch a man's waistline *exceeds* his chest measurement, his life expectancy is reduced by two years. This test measures the endurance strength of the adbominal muscles and is recognized by the International Committee on the Standardization of Physical Fitness Assessments.

How to Score Your Sit-Up Abdominal Strength/Endurance:

MEN

20-29	30-39	40-49	50-59	60-69	Rating	Points
34 +	32 +	31 +	27 +	24 +	*Excellent*	10
31 – 33	29 – 31	27 – 30	23 – 26	20 – 23	*Very Good*	8
27 – 30	25 – 28	23 – 26	19 – 22	16 – 19	*Good*	6
22 – 26	20 – 24	18 – 22	16 – 18	12 – 15	*Fair*	4
19 – 21	16 – 19	14 – 17	13 – 15	9 – 11	*Moderately Low*	2
15 – 18	13 – 15	11 – 13	8 – 12	5 – 8	*Low*	6
0 – 14	0 – 12	0 – 10	0 – 7	0 – 4	*Very Low*	0

WOMEN

20 – 29	30 – 39	40 – 49	50 – 59	60 – 69	Rating	Points
30 +	28 +	25 +	23 +	22 +	*Excellent*	10
26 – 29	24 – 27	21 – 24	20 – 22	18 – 21	*Very Good*	8
22 – 25	20 – 23	17 – 20	16 – 19	14 – 17	*Good*	6
18 – 21	16 – 19	13 – 16	12 – 15	10 – 13	*Fair*	4
14 – 17	12 – 15	10 – 12	8 – 11	7 – 9	*Moderately Low*	2
10 – 13	9 – 11	6 – 9	4 – 7	3 – 6	*Low*	1
0 – 9	0 – 8	0 – 5	0 – 3	0 – 2	*Very Low*	0

• Lie on your back with your knees well bent, feet placed about 15 inches (45 centimetres) from your hips, hands clasped behind your head. Your feet should be firmly held by another person, or placed under something such as the edge of a bed, couch or bureau. Perform as many sit-ups as you can in 30 seconds. Your elbows must touch your knees and your hands must touch the floor on each return.

4. Forward Reach Flexibility Test

Muscle elasticity and full joint range of motion are elements which tend to decline with advancing age and with decreasing fitness levels. On the other hand, full flexibility can encourage the retention of bodily physical youthfulness, reduce the degree of muscle tension to which we are liable and also reduce the chance of muscle and joint injuries resulting from accidents or sports activities.

Two areas which are particularly susceptible to a loss of full mobility as a result of our sedentary living habits are the torso, particularly the low back region, and the muscles and tendons in the backs of the knees and the upper legs. The following test measures your degree of mobility in these two areas.

- Place a 3-foot rule on a box, so that the 12 inch point is in line with the front edge of the box. Sit on the floor, feet touching the front of the box. Keeping the legs perfectly straight, slowly reach forward with both hands. Estimate to the closest half inch how far your fingers can reach along the ruler.

How to Score Your Flexibility:

MEN

20-29	30-39	40-49	50-59	60-69	Rating	Points
20″ or more	19″ or more	18½″ or more	17″ or more	14″ or more	Excellent	10
17″ - 20″	17″ – 19″	16″ – 18½″	15″ – 17″	12″ – 14″	Very Good	8
15″ – 17″	14½″ – 17″	14″ – 16″	12″ – 15″	9½″ – 12″	Good	6
13″ – 15″	12″ – 14½″	11½″ – 14″	10″ – 12″	7″ – 9½″	Fair	4
10½″ – 13″	9½″ – 12″	9½″ – 11½″	7½″ – 10″	5″ – 7″	Moderately Low	2
8″ – 10½″	7½″ – 9½″	7″ – 9″	5″ – 7½″	2″ – 5″	Low	1
less than 8″	less than 7½″	less than 7″	less than 5″	less than 2″	Very Low	0

WOMEN

20-29	30-39	40-49	50-59	60-69	Rating	Points
21″ or more	20½″ or more	20″ or more	19½″ or more	19″ or more	Excellent	10
19″ – 21″	18″ – 20½″	18″ – 20″	17″ – 19½″	16½″ – 19″	Very Good	8
16½″ – 19″	16″ – 18″	15½″ – 18″	14½″ – 17″	14″ – 16½″	Good	6
14½″ – 16½″	14″ – 16″	13½″ – 15½″	12″ – 14½″	12″ – 14″	Fair	4
12″ – 14½″	11½″ – 14″	11″ – 13½″	10″ – 12″	9½″ – 12″	Moderately Low	2
10″ – 12″	9″ – 11½″	8″ – 11″	7½″ – 10″	7″ – 9½″	Low	1
less than 10″	less than 9″	less than 8″	less than 7½″	less than 7″	Very Low	0

5. The 15-Second Push-Up Test

This endurance strength test is also endorsed by the International Committee on the Standardization of Physical Fitness Assessment. Men should use the full push-up but women, the kneeling variation.

●   Lie flat on the floor, arms bent, and then vigorously push up to arms' length. Immediately return to the starting position and do as many push-ups as you can in 15 seconds. Keep your body straight and don't hold your breath.

How to Score Your Upper Body (Push-Up)
Strength/Endurance:

MEN

20 – 29	30 – 39	40 – 49	50 – 59	60 – 69	Rating	Points
24+	22+	20+	19+	17+	*Excellent*	10
21 – 23	19 – 21	17 – 19	16 – 18	13 – 16	*Very Good*	8
18 – 20	15 – 18	14 – 16	12 – 15	10 – 12	*Good*	6
15 – 17	12 – 14	10 – 13	9 – 11	7 – 9	*Fair*	4
11 – 14	9 – 11	7 – 9	5 – 8	4 – 6	*Moderately Low*	2
8 – 10	5 – 8	4 – 6	3 – 4	1 – 3	*Low*	1
0 – 7	0 – 4	0 – 3	0 – 2	0	*Very Low*	0

WOMEN

20 – 29	30 – 39	40 – 49	50 – 59	60 – 69	Rating	Points
21+	19+	17+	17+	16+	*Excellent*	10
18 – 20	16 – 18	14 – 16	13 – 16	13 – 15	*Very Good*	8
15 – 17	12 – 15	11 – 13	10 – 12	10 – 12	*Good*	6
11 – 14	9 – 11	8 – 10	7 – 9	7 – 9	*Fair*	4
8 – 10	6 –8	4 – 7	4 – 6	4 – 6	*Moderately Low*	2
5 – 7	3 – 5	2 – 3	2 – 3	1 – 3	*Low*	1
0 – 4	0 – 2	0 – 1	0 – 1	0	*Very Low*	0

Personal Fitness Profile

Test	Actual Score	Rating	Points
1. Predicted Maximum Oxygen Uptake *(3-Minute Step Test)*			
2. Percent Body Fat			
3. Abdominal Strength /Endurance *(Sit-Ups)*			
4. Flexibility Reach			
5. Upper Body Strength /Endurance *(Push-Ups)*			
	Total Score		100

Determine Your Over-all Fitness Rating

Total Score	Over-all Fitness Rating
90 – 100	*Excellent*
75 – 89	*Very Good*
60 – 74	*Good*
40 – 59	*Fair*
25 – 39	*Moderately Low*
10 – 24	*Low*
0 – 9	*Very Low*

ASSESSMENT BY FITNESS EXPERTS

Pilots are better off having their fitness assessed by experts because the results will be more objective and more accurate.

The best single measurement of fitness is your predicted maximum oxygen capacity. If you tried the advanced fitness assessment in the previous section, you will appreciate the complexities of making even a crude measure of your predicted maximum oxygen uptake. You can have your oxygen uptake and a variety of other fitness measurements assessed at a good fitness club, or possibly a nearby YMCA or hospital.

The essence of fitness is to work and play with energy and with endurance, an ideal achieved by a high level of cardio-respiratory efficiency. This is the ability to supply oxygen to your muscles during physical activity. Working muscles require oxygen for the production of fuel and energy and the elimination of the waste products. Without sufficient oxygen supply to muscles, waste products accumulate and the muscles become fatigued. The transport of oxygen from lungs through the bloodstream to the working muscles is extremely important, and a person's peak capacity is his maximum oxygen uptake. The higher your maximum oxygen uptake (aerobic capacity), the greater will be your physical working capacity. Walking 1 mile (1.6 kilometres) in 10 minutes requires only 1 litre of oxygen per minute above what your resting body needs. Running the same distance in under 8 minutes demands an extra 3 litres per minute! Although oxygen uptake figures can be expressed in litres, they are often converted to the number of millilitres of oxygen per kilogram of body weight per minute. Thus, 2 litres per minute for a person weighing 75 kilograms would convert into 26 ml/kg/min.

The accompanying chart illustrates the effect that your aerobic capacity has on your capacity for activity. Assuming that playing golf requires about 10 millilitres of oxygen per kilogram of body weight per minute, and playing tennis, 30 ml/kg/min., Pilot A who has a maximum oxygen uptake of 20 ml/kg/min. is fit enough to play golf without difficulty — it requires only 50 per cent of his total capacity. Tennis, however, would be too much for him, demanding 50 per cent *more* than his ability to deliver. He would tire quickly.

Oxygen Demand and Supply is the Key . . .

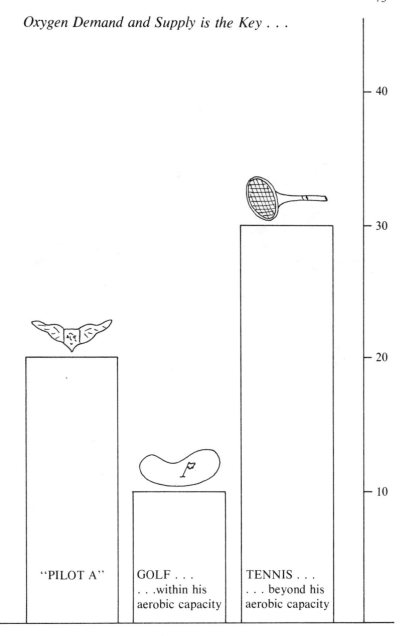

74

This is why when you are out of shape you huff and puff so easily. The activity demands more oxygen than you can deliver; your heart pounds and your lungs heave, and you are forced to quit.

A person's maximum oxygen uptake can be determined, directly or indirectly, by tests involving measured amounts of physical activity during which the individual's oxygen consumption, or pulse rate, is monitored. Such tests usually involve running on a treadmill, cycling on a specially calibrated stationary bicycle or stepping up and down on a box or bench.

Knowing the amount of work done and oxygen consumed (or the after-exercise pulse rate) it is possible to determine or closely predict the number of millilitres of oxygen that can be utilized for every kilogram of body weight per minute.

The accompanying charts indicate fitness levels corresponding to maximum oxygen uptake (Chart 1), how the average maximum oxygen uptake score varies for Canadian men and women of different ages (Chart 2), and how Fitness Institute members score when they first enroll, predicted from bicycle ergometer tests (Chart 3).

CHART 1

Fitness Rating 1

MEN ml/kg/min		WOMEN ml/kg/min
55 + over	Superior	52 + over
50 – 54	Excellent	47 – 51
45 – 49	Very Good	42 – 46
40 – 44	Good	37 – 41
35 – 39	Fair	32 – 36
30 – 34	Low	27 – 31
29 or less	Very Low	26 or less

Note: The above figures are absolute, not age-related, values. It should be recognized that the maximum oxygen uptake tends to decrease as age increases. A "fair" score for a 25 year-old might represent a "very good" score for a 55 or 60-year-old.

CHART 2

Average Maximum Oxygen Uptake Levels for Canadian Men and Women

MEN	AGE	WOMEN
36.4 ml/kg/min	20 – 29	30.6 ml/kg/min
32.6	30 – 39	27.8
26.9	40 – 49	24.3
25.7	50 – 59	21.9
22.8	60 – 69	19.0

The above figures are predicted values and are taken from a study conducted in Saskatoon in 1973. Over 1,200 Canadians were tested and a report on this study was published in the *Canadian Medical Association Journal* (July 6, 1974).

CHART 3

Average Predicted VO² Max Value For Fitness Institute Members (Initial Testing upon Enrolment)

MEN	AGE	WOMEN
42.1 ml/kg/min	20-29	37.5 ml/kg/min
35.9 ml/kg/min	30-39	34.9 ml/kg/min
32.7 ml/kg/min	40-49	31.2 ml/kg/min
29.6 ml/kg/min	50-59	31.3 ml/kg/min
29.5 ml/kg/min	60-69	22.6 ml/kg/min

Regardless of which test is used – treadmill, bicycle, or step – it should include a progressive exercise load. In a sub-maximal test the effort should be continued for at least three minutes at each of three or more workloads, such as increased resistances on the bicycle ergometer. For safety and comfort, the pulse rate is raised to no more than approximately 85 per cent of the predicted maximum. A maximal test is more accurate, but a doctor should attend while the subject is given increasing workloads until he is taken to his physiological limits (his heart rate levels off despite the increasing workload) or has to stop because of muscular fatigue, pain, dizziness or other problem. Often, in the maximal test, air expelled by the

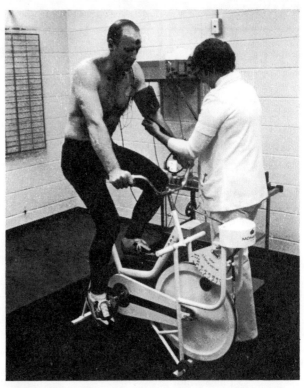

subject is collected and analysed to determine exactly how much oxygen was utilized.

The typical sub-maximal test assumes that the oxygen consumption and heart rate relationship is constant. The pulse rate should be raised to at least 120 beats per minute to permit a reasonably reliable result. It should not exceed 170 beats for those in their 20s or 140 beats per minute for those in their 60s. At higher workloads, however, the effects of such non-exercise factors as anxiety are greatly reduced. The body has natural mechanisms to protect it from reaching exertion danger levels. The rare occurrence of a person dying during or after exercise sometimes receives wide publicity, but a close examination of the facts usually reveals substantial heart disease or an inadequate pre-assessment medical. There are advantages, however, in not reaching exhaustion. For one, it's not a pleasant experience. Secondly, most comparison tables are based on sub-maximal predicted oxygen uptake values.

And thirdly, when a person is pushed to his limits, especially in a bicycle test, his leg muscles may fatigue before his heart, lungs and circulatory systems reach their maximum output, thereby making it more a test of leg strength and endurance than aerobic efficiency.

Under normal circumstances, your pulse rate is an accurate indicator of the volume of oxygen needed for the muscular work you are performing. The more intense the work, the higher the oxygen demand, and therefore the faster the pulse rate. By adjusting the workloads (the resistance on the ergometer or angle and speed of the treadmill), each person being tested can be brought to approximately the same pulse rate level. This is a safer method than comparing the different pulse rates of individuals who are given a standard workload such as running a mile in 10 minutes. Such a test might push an unfit person's pulse rate to an extremely high level.

Apprehension about the test can raise your pulse rate and affect your score. While it would be truthful to advise you that there is nothing to worry about, the best way to ensure a reliable score is to go through a trial run a few days before your first test.

The test should be done in a quiet place at a temperature near 20 degrees Celsius. A small fan will move the air around your body, and a metronome will help you keep the proper stepping or cycling pace. Stethoscope and manual measurements of accelerated pulse rates are inferior to electrocardiograms. The ECG gives an accurate reading and has the second advantage of describing the condition of the heart under stress. At the first sign of an abnormal condition a tester will abort the test.

Because weight is a factor in calculating oxygen uptake, it is obvious that an overweight pilot will have a lower score than if he was a lesser poundage. Simply losing weight will improve his score. In effect, he will have the same sized engine powering a lighter aircraft.

Finally, no perfect sub-maximal oxygen uptake measuring system has been devised. The score obtained on a treadmill will usually be approximately 7 per cent higher than that obtained on a bicycle ergometer. Running or cycling skill, leg power and motivation also contribute to the imperfection of measuring. That is not to say these tests are a waste of time. Valuable judgments about your fitness can be made by comparing yourself with others of your sex and age group who use the same test procedures. You can also gauge your heart-respiratory improvement in future re-tests.

REASSESSMENT

If, after going through your fitness assessment, you discover that you are out of shape, you are not alone. Only 20 per cent of all Canadians over 14 years of age spend one hour per week or more of their leisure time doing some form of physical exercise. On the other hand, 85 per cent of Canadians watch at least 15 hours of television each week. Further, fewer than 2 per cent of Canadians exercise regularly.

Measurement adds interest, confidence and motivation to your fitness program. One advantage of our recommended program is that you can measure your progress daily. This will allow you to predict with some accuracy the results of a reassessment which should be done at regular intervals. It is more important to be reassessed if you choose alternative fitness sports or recreation programs because most don't tell you where you're at each day.

Keep your test results and fitness rating for future reference. After six weeks on your exercise program, do another assessment. If you have been conscientious in your workouts, expect a pleasant surprise. Initial improvements are often dramatic. Exercising for fitness improvement is like climbing a mountain. Lots of ground is covered quickly and easily near the base. As you climb higher, progress becomes slower. This can be a difficult period, a time when many give up. Patience and persistence are essential. Near the top, each step is slower, more difficult. Usually, only highly motivated athletes and fitness fanatics stand on the pinnacle of fitness. Fortunately, it isn't essential to reach the top. If you achieve the three-quarter or even halfway level, you will be reaping the benefits of fitness. If you have had a professional assessment, aim to repeat the procedure periodically, at least once every year, to monitor your progress or simply show that you are maintaining an adequate level of fitness. In addition, try the "home use" test described in this book, perhaps once every three months. Reassessments not only reveal your improvements, they indicate what modifications are needed in exercise procedure. No pill will improve physical fitness. It takes long and consistent effort to transform a sedentary body into one that is strong and fit.

Pre-Fitness Checks

> . . . fill the unforgiving minute with
> sixty seconds' worth of distance
> run . . . – Rudyard Kipling

A useful pilot fitness program isn't easy; it can't be completed in a mere 30 minutes a week. No one gets in shape being lazy. Books announcing the ease of attaining fitness are fraudulent, designed to sell themselves, not fitness. They promise riches without rigour, the proverbial something for nothing.

Fitness is a way of life, not a two-week enthusiasm for physical routines. After all, it has taken your total previous life to put your body in its present shape. If that has been a sedentary history, it can't be wiped out with a few push-ups. Surprisingly, though, changes are felt almost immediately upon launching a fitness program that contains variety, challenge, and the means of measuring progress against your former self and others.

Just as a good program isn't easy, it shouldn't be too tough. The road to fitness is cluttered with those who break down because they start too fast. They run into stiff muscles and shattered expectations. Good planning is essential; your goal and plans must be suited to what you are, not what you hope you are.

Aim to have an all-round program. Jogging is good for the legs, heart and lungs, but does nothing for upper body strength and flexibility. Weight training builds muscle and strength, but does little for endurance. Even swimming, one of the best all-round activities, won't help much to improve your flexibility, balance and agility. A good program will tax all muscles (stretching and stressing them to a safe limit), involve movements of joints through their full range, reduce adrenal products in the blood, exercise the cardio-respiratory system, help your balance and coordination, and include methods to achieve a release of tension. Your program should be progressive in its demands, yet molded to your strengths, weaknesses, likes and dislikes. Work for success and personal satisfaction, but don't be drawn into the trap of always striving for more. When you have achieved your long-range goals, switch to a maintenance program which contains continuing personal rewards and frequent reassessments so your fitness level doesn't slide back.

Your program and individual daily workouts should be characterized by an attitude of "relaxed concentration." A champion runner or basketball player makes his winning performance look easy because he applies the power of relaxation. Being tense is a sign that muscles are working against each other instead of in harmony.

Boredom and lack of motivation are major failings in the fitness movement. If you can make your program fun, challenging and interesting, you will have more chance of success. Following are some ideas to consider in designing or choosing a fitness program.

THE EXERCISE ENVIRONMENT

Muscles don't have eyes. They respond to the stresses placed upon them, whether they are working in a plush gymnasium or dingy basement. It is possible to advance your fitness in any environment that is not restrictive or hostile. But the environment can affect your attitude to fitness, and it is important that your attitude remain buoyant to the last exercise. You will soon grow tired if exercising is a puritanical and grey experience. The options for a fitness environment are numerous and you should select the one(s) suited to your needs and personality. You can join a recreation fitness group, a community sports organization (such as a jogging, squash or hiking group), or a fitness club. Or you may join a friend or two who have the same interest and goals. Others provide motivation and distraction from repetitious routines. There is a special camaraderie, an instant rapport, a community of fitness and ready-made conversations among joggers, tennis players and others. And with a partner it isn't easy to hide a roll of fat or the gasping breath during what should be an easy warm-up jog. You can't so easily cancel a workout if you're committed to meeting a partner.

If you choose to do it on your own at home, find or make for yourself a clean, well-lighted, large space with a carpeted floor. Watching television or listening to the radio can ease the monotony of repetitious exercises. Music reduces the sensation of labour. Music and physical movement have many parallels; both are temporal and can be rhythmic, inspiring and beautiful. Just as a guitarist taps his foot for proper cadence, the pilot can use music to keep good pace in his calisthenics or stationary cycling. Knowing how many minutes your favourite music lasts, aim to do your final cool-off exercise with the last bar. Exercise your way through your entire record library, avoiding the excessive pulse rate of rock and inadequate effort inherent in slow classical music.

Fitness is one of those best things in life that is free. Much home gymnasium equipment is unnecessary. With a little imagination, you can substitute for exercises which require equipment. Too often, equipment is purchased moments after a person has suddenly decided to get fit, and after a few feverish workouts the apparatus is abandoned. The cost of jogging and calisthenics is only time and effort. On the other hand, a small mat will make your exercises more comfortable and a low (18 inches), 5-foot-long backless bench may be handy for some exercises. If you are a big spender, consider equipment such as an exercise bicycle or rowing machine that will work the big muscles of the body.

Some health spas and commercial fitness centres are justifiably criticized by fitness experts for selling the myth that weight loss, good muscles, appearance and health can be purchased. The setting for their sales pitch may include vibrators, chrome-plated barbells, tinted mirrors, marbled saunas and plush carpets. They sometimes lack trained personnel and intelligent programs, and their membership contracts waive their liability if you are injured or over-stressed while on their premises. These places emphasize weight training, the building of the body for the sake of cosmetic appearance, and give barely a passing nod at essential aerobic conditioning. What they offer is of questionable value. For instance, it has been calculated that it would require 15 minutes of vibrator massaging each day for a whole year to lose one pound of body fat.

While doing a fitness routine on your own allows you to do exactly what you want when you want, usually with less travelling, waiting and expense, don't quickly discard the advantages of working out with others, even in a private health club. A well-administered fitness club which includes many recreational activities can offer the best environment to achieve rapid progress. Even a $500 or $700 annual membership is worth it if you know you would never do it on your own, or you are uncertain about your fitness goals and program content. The cost of *not* being fit is invariably higher than the most expensive fee at a good club.

FITNESS CLOTHING

Good footwear and clothing protects you from a hot, cold or wet environment. With proper clothing you can cross-country ski or jog outdoors in some of the coldest weather. One-third of your body heat escapes via your head, so wear a hat on such days. When your head is covered, flimsily covered hands and feet have a better chance of staying warm. But why take a chance? Cover everything well. Mittens are better than gloves because fingers help keep each other warm. If you are skiing, loose fitting boots are better than cutting off the circulation in your feet with two or three pairs of heavy socks. Cross-country skiers sometimes wear socks over their boots to reduce the chill. In extremely cold temperatures and strong winds, a balaclava covers ears, nose and cheeks which might otherwise be devastated by frostbite. It's impossible to frostbite your lungs, but extremely cold air can make your chest uncomfortable and make you feel short of breath. A surgical mask or loose fitting scarf a few inches from your mouth stops the cold rush.

Plastic bags around the feet, and plastic clothing in general, are not recommended because they prevent moisture loss. The increasing volume of trapped perspiration can't be kept warm and eventually the body is chilled. Recommended is fishnet underwear covered by one or more thin layers of woollen clothing – a combination that traps dead air next to the skin for insulation but allows the escape of some moisture. A heavy jacket unfortunately gives you only the option of being too hot or, if you take it off, too cold. A light, loose-fitting windbreaker is less cumbersome and ideal as the outer layer. If you're jogging outside at night, wear white clothing or put some reflective tape on your outfit. Of course, the amount of clothing you need depends on the task undertaken. Speed produces heat and reduces the need for clothing. On a long, slow, winter hike or cross-country ski tour wear heavier clothing with polyester fiber-fill or down. The warmth will prevent muscle pulls and improve physical condition.

Warm clothing will not replace the need for warm-up exercises. A warm-up prepares your heart and circulation system and, unlike clothing, warms your muscles from the inside out.

Once having started your activities in the cold outdoors, don't stop too long to rest, unless at a warming station. Sweat dries rapidly and resulting chill can mean you won't get warm again. Plan to end at a place where you can stay warm, have a shower and change into dry clothing.

The right amount and type of clothing will allow you to maintain a normal 98.6 degrees Fahrenheit body temperature. Wearing a sweat suit on hot days (possibly for reasons of modesty) can be just as foolish as not wearing one on cold days (possibly for reasons of looking 'cool'). Long underwear, disguised by dye to look like ballet tights, worn under track shorts is an excellent combination for jogging on cool spring or fall days – if you are prepared to ignore a comment or two from onlookers. On hot days wear a cap to shade your eyes and cover the back of your head.

FREQUENCY

Fitness cannot be stored. Some former athletes, particularly those in skill-dominant (as opposed to endurance) sports, may hold a vague hope that their sports careers have rendered them immune to future heart attacks. But the body does not thrive on memories; blood, not glory, is being pumped through its veins and arteries. Former gridiron heroes, especially overweight linemen who now do no exercise, can be more susceptible to heart attack than physically inactive persons of average weight.

Fitness must be restored. Frequently. Make physical exercise a daily habit. Even if you don't have a scheduled workout, do something to step up your heart rate for 15 to 30 minutes, such as mowing the grass (non-motorized mowers are best) or taking a walk. You start to become de-conditioned within three days of a good workout, so schedule exercise at least every second day. If you set aside time every day for exercising, you will never have to ask yourself, "Should I exercise today or put it off until tomorrow?" Fitness becomes a habit as integral to your life as eating and sleeping. A brief workout is an excellent break from a busy day or if you have a few hours between flights. Some fitness authorities say that if you can't exercise regularly, you shouldn't exercise at all. Certainly, sporadic exercise is dangerous if it's especially taxing. But done in moderation, it is better than none at all. Some pilots cannot be regular exercisers because of family or flight schedules. The pilot who consistently offers the excuse that he has too little time for fitness should examine his priorities and the benefits of fitness.

For every day you miss, count back the same number of days from where you left off your program and restart there. If you miss more than 14 days, start your program again from the beginning.

MORNING, NOON OR NIGHT?

It doesn't matter too much what time of day you set aside for exercising. When possible, do your program at the same time each day so you will have the same recovery period between workouts. Pick a time that suits your temperament, lifestyle and work schedule. Exercising immediately before a scheduled meal will dull your appetite – a benefit to dieters. Exercising moments after you eat is not recommended. Indigestion and nausea are caused by the conflicting demand for blood by the active muscles and digestive system. Wait an hour or two. A mild workout before bedtime may help you relax, but most programs will raise your heart rate and stimulate other body processes, making sleep more difficult. Some people think they do better in the morning. The President's Council on Fitness in the United States made the interesting discovery that the most dedicated fitness practitioners exercise early in the morning. They just can't wait to start! A pre-breakfast jog may leave you tired because your blood sugar level has dropped during the night. Drinking orange juice before your pre-breakfast exercise can leave your stomach too acidic, causing cramps, even vomiting.

If you are in the habit of having one or two alcoholic drinks on non-flight days, don't drink until after a workout. Drinking stresses the heart and impairs judgment needed during your routines, such as deciding when you have done enough and avoiding risks to physical safety.

Daily exercise heightens mental alertness, as long as it is accompanied by sufficient rest. A 10 mile (16 kilometre) jog before a long flight is not recommended, but a brief workout is desirable. Cockpit drills, described later, help relieve boredom, fatigue, and other stresses including backache on medium and long flights. Get the whole crew doing them – they may be bored and fatigued too! After a flight and on lay-overs, a brisk workout is often more restorative than a mid-day sleep.

ELEMENTS OF A GOOD PILOT FITNESS PROGRAM

Be wary of adopting a fitness program made for the masses. Choose or create one suited to your goals, needs, fitness assessment and personal preferences. A variety of programs, including a recommended program which contains numerous options, is described in the following chapters. A good fitness club will help you design a program. Some clubs will design a home program for a small fee, and it is not conditional upon your becoming a club member. The most important ingredient in your program will be the motivation to do it again tomorrow. A change of environment, exercise program or training partner may aid this motivation, as long as consistency and progression of effort are maintained. If you change programs as often as your undershirt, progress will be retarded and you can expect to have sore muscles. Each exercise or sport uses specific muscles in specific ways, so it takes weeks for them to become accustomed to new stresses, however slight the difference. A fitness log is a good motivational aid. Record workout details and related information such as body weight and waist measurement.

As noted previously, the emphasis in a sound program should be on the development of cardiovascular fitness, achieved by extended and vigorous activity involving the large muscles of the body. Walking, jogging, cycling, swimming, cross-country skiing, hiking and rowing are popular cardiovascular exercises. They are described as aerobic – powered by a steady and adequate oxygen supply. Exercises which demand more oxygen than the body can supply in a short time (it happens to a runner who sprints all out for 300 metres) are anaerobic – carried out in the absence of sufficient oxygen. Anaerobic exercises alone are not effective in conditioning the heart-circulatory and respiratory systems because muscles are fatigued before a sufficient training effect is achieved.

When choosing the type and intensity of aerobic exercise, it is safer to do too little than too much. Like infants, sedentary pilots should walk before they run. So, if your assessment shows that you're in poor shape, start walking! Go at a slow pace and add a minute or two each day. Try to progress slowly. Your body has an optimum rate of adjustment to exercise which should not be challenged by fatiguing, strenuous work. Effective exercise will make you breathe deeply and perspire. A more accurate measure of exercise intensity is calorie expenditure and the stress imposed on the heart and lungs. A simple evaluation of intensity can be obtained from the pulse rate. Out-of-condition pilots will receive a "training effect" from heart rates of 100 to 130 beats per minute. After a few weeks of exercises, the intensity should be raised so that the heart is pumping at 70 to 80 per cent of the pilot's estimated maximum. Heart rate maximums decrease with age. The maximum rate of a 50-year-old man or woman is about 20 beats per minute below that of a 30-year-old. This helps explain why older individuals are not able to exercise as strenuously as younger people. The accompanying figures indicate age-predicted heart rates and target exercise heart rates for adult age groups.

To gain a training effect the target heart rate must be sustained for 20 to 30 minutes in each workout, either as a continuous effort or the cumulative time of a series of efforts. For example, an excellent workout for a moderately fit pilot would consist of seven times a 450 to 500-metre run, each taking 3 minutes to complete. For the duration of each run, his heart would be pumping at the target rate.

87

Approximate Maximum Heart Rates by Age and Recommended Training Heart Rates

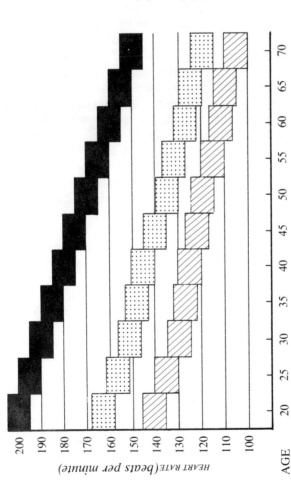

The range representing
the predicted maximum
heart rate.

The range representing
approximately 80 per cent
of the predicted maximum
heart rate.

The range representing
approximately 70 per cent
of the predicted maximum
heart rate.

The chart graphically depicts how the maximum heart rate declines with increasing age. The black area indicates the range of the predicted maximum heart rate for each age group. Recommended training heart rates are shown by the shaded areas. The cross-hatch area indicates the range representing approximately 70 per cent of the estimated maximum heart rate which is a relatively mild level of training intensity. The dotted area representing approximately 80 per cent of the maximum defines a more ideal training intensity.

Between each run there would be a recovery period of 1 to 2 minutes, at which time the heart would return to a rate far below the target tempo.

After you have reached a medium level of fitness you could run or cycle continuously for 30 minutes three times a week to maintain minimum fitness. That's less than 1 per cent of your life's time, a small investment for a big dividend. Those who exercise most often and regularly reap the greatest benefits. It is best to alternate stressful workouts, such as described above, with an easy exercise day. Do no more than three stressful workouts each week, and never do two on successive days. An unbroken string of hard workout days will wear you down and take you further away instead of closer to your goal. And one hard workout followed by six days of inactivity will not make you fit. It could be dangerous. One thing a weekend athlete can count on: he will probably die on a weekend.

Constant monitoring of your pulse – taken manually at one side of your neck – is probably the best method of determining whether you are achieving the target rate and therefore bearing an appropriate exercise workload. Another check which can be made after the last exercise of your program is to find your heart recovery time. Your pulse should return close to normal resting levels in 10 minutes. If after 5 minutes it is still above 120 you are probably doing too much.

When training with others, don't let competition obscure good sense. Running faster or lifting more weights than a partner may push your heart rate too high. Train with, not against, others. Exercise overload is signalled by the onset of considerable discomfort. "Fatigue acids" build up in your muscles, telling you to slow down. Regular exercises will improve your tolerance to fatigue, but guard against pushing yourself to a maximum heart rate. Your pulse rate indicates the amount of work you are doing and your heart's efficiency. As your fitness improves, your heart will work less (pulse rate will go down) to perform a standard workload. Therefore, you will have to increase the workload to maintain a target heart rate. Besides boosting your capacity for work, your improved fitness will give you a lower resting pulse rate. Your heart will do less work to get you through each day. A reduction of 5 or more beats per minute after the first six weeks to three months of an initial fitness program is not too much to expect.

Prolonged cardiovascular exercise will cause the loss of a significant amount of body moisture through perspiration and respiration. About four-fifths of blood is water. When water in the blood and muscles is reduced by exercise, delivering nutrients such as fats and glucose to the muscles and removing lactate and carbon dioxide is inhibited. The myth that drinking during exercise is bad for you has no logical foundation, unless the drink is alcoholic. For every percentage point of liquid body weight loss you can add a zero and that's your percentage loss of exercise efficiency. For example, if you lose 2 per cent in liquid body weight, you will lose 20 per cent efficiency. If you feel thirsty during your program replace your fluid loss by drinking small quantities of water. Fruit juices can cause stomach cramps. Sugared solutions delay the absorption of liquid through the stomach, but do eventually help to raise the blood sugar levels which are depleted rapidly in strenuous exercise.

Besides nourishing the working muscles, the circulatory system brings exercise-generated heat to the skin where it's expelled. When the circulatory system can't keep up – because it's being depleted of water, the atmospheric temperature is too high, or the person is wearing too many clothes – the body temperature begins to rise. Long-distance runners have recorded body temperatures of 104 degrees Fahrenheit or more running on hot days. Besides taking frequent drinks of water, keep your body cool by jogging on the shady side of the street, wearing reflective clothing, exercising at the cool times of the day and following your workout with a cool shower, not a sauna. What cannot be restored during a cardiovascular workout is glycogen, the glucose stored in the muscles. It can take almost two days to replenish the glycogen stores after an especially demanding workout. Carbohydrates are the chief source of glycogen and endurance athletes therefore emphasize carbohydrates in their diets. Following several days of exercising and profuse sweating, you may experience muscle cramps because of a loss of electrolytes such as potassium and sodium. A little extra salt with your meals should correct the imbalance.

The impression shouldn't be made here that muscular strength is unimportant, a mere liability in this age when a big test of power is to twist the lid off the children's peanut butter jar. Good muscles improve your sports ability, appearance and posture and prevent injuries and premature fatigue. Muscular strength is especially important in the abdominal and lower back areas which are so vulnerable to ruin in middle-aged sedentary people. Muscles support the body structure. Their tone, flexibility and strength influence your health, well-being, metabolism, and emotional state. And, a fact sometimes overlooked, they help keep your heart and circulatory system in sound condition and also provide life-maintaining energy. Bodily distortions that occur (and are too readily accepted) with aging are not always deposits of excess fat: they may be unused, weak muscles that are failing to do their intended support job. Unfortunately, few medical examinations take cognizance of the importance of muscular condition. Sometimes pills are prescribed for patients who would do better on a new diet of muscle-building exercises.

While the need for strength is unquestionable, some methods of obtaining it should be questioned. Generally, there are two kinds of exercises for muscle groups – ryhthmic and static. The rhythmic exercises are those, such as jogging and swimming, that involve repetition and endurance: blood flow is promoted. Static exercises are characterized by bursts of power and little or no movement at all – just human muscle pushing violently against an immovable object: blood circulation is restricted. These Charles Atlas techniques build muscle bulk and increase blood pressure without compensating benefits to the heart. Blood pressure rises during exercise and often goes higher when smaller muscles are used. It is measurably higher for arm than leg work. Lifting heavy weights above your head can raise the blood pressure too high (and can injure your back).

An essential ingredient in a comprehensive program is flexibility exercises, often done during the warm-up. Stretching reduces resistance inherent in muscle tissues. Coaches and physical educators in recent years have favoured the "static" stretch; each large muscle group is stretched to its limit and held for a few seconds. Dogs and cats do it naturally. Rapid "ballistic" stretching (an example is alternate toe touching) can cause muscle spasm and create more tension. The static stretch produces the flexibility to perform your physical skills more easily, possibly faster and with less muscle soreness later. Post-exercise soreness was once thought to be caused by tiny ruptures of muscle tissues. Now, researchers believe it may result from the failure of muscles to relax during exercise and that means they have been deprived of blood. To remove the pain and spasm, a muscle should be stretched.

During (if possible) and after a long flight, pilots should routinely do some static stretches, especially for the hamstring (back of thigh) muscles which have been shortened and bunched from long hours of sitting. Muscle elasticity and range-of-motion in the joints decline with advancing age and decreasing fitness. Flexibility exercises will help you maintain your youthfulness and prevent injuries, particularly in the torso and back of the legs and knees. In designing your program, top priority should be given leg exercises. Leg and buttock muscles are the largest, and when in use, they create strong demands on the heart and lungs. There is truth to the axiom: if you want to know the condition of a man's heart, feel his leg muscles.

Another vital program element is simplicity. Concentrate on a few exercises such as jogging in summer and cross-country skiing in winter to develop the techniques and specific muscle power to reach a high level of efficiency. Doing a different activity every day means that you will spend more effort learning or relearning skills than properly stressing your cardio-respiratory and muscular structures and you will be vulnerable to injuries, including the annoying little ones such as blisters, bruised heel bones and soreness around the joints. Most disciplines are not complementary. The slow pace of jogging, for instance, can be a detriment to playing tennis where fast responses heighten the enjoyment of the game.

The cardio-respiratory benefit of each activity is roughly proportionate to calorie consumption. So if you choose the excellent sport of cross-country skiing, you will aid both your health and weight loss programs to approximately the same degree. The accompanying lists categorize the potential for achieving exercise and calories loss. Choose the highest fitness-potential exercises that you can comfortably perform. For instance, if you have no special favourite in skiing, select cross-country over downhill. Of course, our list is arbitrary. A lazy soccer player will receive less benefit than a baseball outfielder who jogs on the spot between pitches. These lists rate the exercise, not the exerciser. And it is not a comment on other potential advantages of these activities such as recreational value, personal challenge, release of emotions, and companionship.

Omitted from these lists is sexual intercourse, an activity which can raise the pulse to 140 or more beats a minute. Undoubtedly it has

92

High Potential	Medium Potential	Low Potential
athletics (running 400 metres and longer distances)	athletics (sprints and field events)	archery
ballet	badminton	baseball
basketball	dancing (high tempo)	billiards
boxing (not recommended)	downhill skiing	bowling
cross-country skiing	figure skating	cricket
cycling	gymnastics	curling
field hockey	hiking	double tennis
ice hockey	lawn mowing (non-motorized mower)	gardening
knee bends (half squats)	recreational canoeing	golf
		horse riding
orienteering	singles tennis	lawn bowling
rowing	stair walking	lawn mowing (motorized mower, no seat)
rugby	touch football	sailing
running (jogging) distances	volleyball	
		snowmobiling
soccer		table tennis
speed skating		volleyball
squash		walking (slow pace)
stair running	swimming distances	

some exercise benefit but it's hardly something we can suggest as a progressive program. Probably few of us will interrupt coitus to record our pulse. Heart rates during sex are elevated as much from adrenalin as exercise, so the fast rate isn't even an accurate measure of activity. A sound exercise program will allow you to enjoy sex more.

A good fitness program also contains warm-up, cool-off and flexibility routines. A full explanation of these elements is contained in the next chapter. No matter if you are following the recommended program or an alternate plan, leave time and energy for these transitory factors in fitness, the warm-up taking you from an inactive to an active state, flexibility from limited physical movement to the full range of movement, and the cool-off from the active back to the resting state.

SICKNESS AND INJURY

A bonus by-product of exercising will be the reduction of your susceptibility to certain sicknesses and injuries. Of course, fitness is no iron-clad guarantee of freedom from disease and injury, which may from time to time force you to postpone your program. During the convalescence you will lose the training effects rapidly, particularly if you are confined to bed or have some part of your body wrapped in a cast. It will take one to two days of exercising for each day you were laid off to restore your former condition. For instance, if you miss one week because of the flu, it will take up to two weeks after you have recovered to reach your previous level of fitness. Pamper yourself, but not for long. There are as many disadvantages in returning to your program too late as too early after an illness or injury. Restart slowly to avoid sore and stiff muscles.

The chance of injury increases with fatigue, such as in the last few minutes of a workout when tiredness can interfere with coordination and concentration. Forget the finishing sprint. Some tired joggers twist ankles; some tired cross-country skiers fall or run into trees; and some tired gymnasts fall from the parallel bars. Injuries are also more prevalent in those learning a new skill; so be cautious and when possible obtain professional instruction. Poor equipment, shoes and clothing can cause injuries. Buy new shoes long before your feet show through the soles of the old ones. A host of orthopedic injuries can be avoided by using proper footwear.

Muscles starved of blood become fatigued and are susceptible to cramps. The deprivation of blood can be caused by atherosclerotic clogging of vessels, prolonged and unaccustomed exercise, or cold temperatures. Cramps most often occur in feet and legs. Slow stretching of the cramped area and rest should relieve the seizure. Physiotherapy and diet manipulation may be the cure for chronic cramps but should be used only after advice from a physician. Local heat aids blood flow and may be helpful. Saunas are not an answer. They promote a feeling of relaxation and may help cleanse the skin, but have no true fitness, health, weight-loss, or therapeutic benefits.

Foot, ankle and shin damage is common in joggers and those whose programs involve running. It can be avoided by employing a proper warm-up, exercise techniques, equipment and footwear. If you can't find a grassy or soft surface, put plenty of cushion between your feet and the ground you are running on. If that doesn't help relieve the pain, slow down or stop altogether until you are healed. If everything, including rest, fails, consider switching to swimming, cycling or cross-country skiing which are easier on the joints, bones and muscles in your legs and feet.

Epicondylitis, better known as tennis elbow, is caused by racquet ball, tennis, squash and handball, and other arm activities. A chief cause is the improperly performed backhand stroke. The repeated motion inflames the tendons. Cures range from long-term rest, cortisone injections, elastic support bandages, and physiotherapy to surgery.

Good posture habits in exercise and non-exercise hours keep stresses on bones, joints, muscles, ligaments and internal organs at a minimum. A brief description of posture exercises is included in a later chapter.

Eyes receive some natural protection from their bony sockets, eyelids and nose, but still they can be damaged by a ball or misplaced racquet or elbow. Because good sight is so vital to a pilot's career, he should not expose his eyes to any danger. A variety of eye protectors and face masks can be purchased. If you wear glasses, use a pair with safety lenses and frames during your fitness activities.

One way to avoid injuries, particularly of the eye, is to refuse to participate in contact activities such as football. A mild, indirect blow can cause internal bleeding in the eye. If you see blood in a portion of your eye, see an opthamologist immediately. Even a slight movement can worsen the bleeding, so remain as still as possible. If there is swelling around the eyes, a small ice pack will reduce it. Don't put pressure on the eye, and, if an abrasion is suspected, it is folly for anyone but a doctor to attempt treatment.

To protect your ears in the swimming pool use a silicone preparation or a bathing cap. Ear infections are sometimes related to bad colds, throat infections and sinusitis, so closely monitor these infections.

8 Recommended Pilot Program

It's not the men in my life that matter;
it's the life in my men – Mae West

One problem facing people eager to get started on an exercise program is knowing what exercises to do, and how much and how often to do them. Some take on vigorous programs which require more time and energy than they can afford. While many routes can be followed to upgrade fitness, we believe that carefully selected exercises, performed frequently, are most desirable. A disciplined, consistent routine is necessary for the most satisfactory results. Our recommended program cannot be hampered by inclement weather or the lack of a partner and facilities such as a pool or tennis court. In addition, it is suitable for both men and women and it allows for progression from a relatively easy starting point to higher degrees of effort and fitness.

Each of the programs outlined in this chapter consists of a warm-up, an optional strength segment, a conditioning routine, and a cool-off. Ideally, the entire program should be performed each time you have a workout. The strength exercises, however, are grouped together as an "optional" segment so that, occasionally, they can be omitted without unduly affecting the balance of the program. Whether you do the entire program or just the conditioning circuit, always do warm-up and cool-off drills.

1. The Warm-up

The warm-up involves stretching movements, abdominal exercises, and drills which gradually accelerate the circulatory and respiratory processes. It is never wise to race a cold engine or a cold human body. A warm-up increases body temperature, enables you to deliver more oxygen to the muscles, and reduces the viscosity of the fluid in the muscles, making it easier for them to contract and relax, and thus reducing the possibility of strain or injury. Static-stretch exercises alone are not complete warm-up exercises because they don't heat muscle tissue or inspire sufficient circulatory response. A proper warm-up may help prevent heart irregularities during exercise. Tests conducted on several athletes showed that when they performed vigorous physical activity without a warm-up, more than half had abnormal electrocardiographic changes. With a warm-up, all of their ECG abnormalities were avoided. The warm-up will take 5 to 10 minutes.

2. Optional Strength Exercises

Building and maintaining muscle strength should be done frequently, but, when time is short, can be reduced or eliminated. Muscle strength makes physically demanding tasks easier to perform, can improve posture, aids performance in sports and recreation, and can affect your morale and confidence.

The strength exercises are primarily for arms, shoulders, back and abdominal muscles. Your legs will receive sufficient strength training in the fitness circuit part of the program. Strength is improved rapidly using heavy resistance equipment such as barbells and pulley weights, but exercises – as suggested in our program – which require no equipment (your body weight and muscle strength serve as the resistance) are effective and can be done at home or on the road.

The most widely used non-equipment strength exercises are "isometrics" which involve the principle of an irresistible force against an immovable object. Muscles contract to near their maximum. An example is pushing one hand hard against the equal force of the other. While isometrics are effective strength builders, they are not recommended for those with blood pressure problems. Isometrics reduce the circulatory flow through the working muscles. We recommend exercises which strengthen muscles through their full operational range and not just at single, fixed positions as in static isometrics.

Female pilots should not assume that strength exercises are only for men. Fear that they will develop bulgy muscles is unfounded. Hormonal differences and a naturally heavier subcutaneous layer of fatty tissue protect women from developing a bulky, muscular appearance. Strength exercises can lead to more attractive appearance for women and men.

3. The Fitness Circuit

The fitness circuit is the key portion of the training program. It improves your cardio-respiratory fitness. Each fitness circuit is a series of exercises which are performed with little or no rest between them. When the last exercise is completed, work through the whole series again. Complete as many circuits as possible in the prescribed time while not exceeding your recommended training heart rate level. Circuit training is adaptable to specific goals. The circuits will give you aerobic benefits equal to what you would receive from jogging or swimming, with the added advantages of improved agility, mobility, balance and muscle strength.

As previously explained, to obtain a training effect you must raise your heart rate to from 60 to 80 per cent of your maximum heart rate and maintain that level for at least 15 minutes. If you are out of condition, however, a lower heart rate for a shorter period of exercising will still help.

Some of the programs, Level 1 for example, begin with short circuits, mild starting points for less-fit pilots. Circuits are gradually increased to 16, then 24 minutes. In the first stages the circuits are broken into two segments of equal duration. Eventually, you will progress to doing the circuit in one uninterrupted session of 20 to 30 minutes.

The procedure recommended in these programs is to complete as many trips through the circuit as possible within the suggested time period but without exceeding your training heart rate. Careful timing and counting is necessary. If possible, do your circuit near a large clock with a sweep second hand. Exercise at a steady, moderate pace. You may stop for brief rests either after or even part way through an exercise. Obviously, however, the more often or the longer you rest, the fewer total repetitions you will complete. Avoid a breakneck pace. It is a training session, not a record-breaking competition! Perform each exercise correctly. Don't cut corners.

Watch your progress by keeping a record of your total number of exercises each day. Simply note the number of full circuits, plus additional exercises completed. For example, two circuits plus three exercises is scored 2/3.

Immediately check your pulse rate at the conclusion of each circuit to make certain it is within the training heart rate range suggested for your program. If it is low, work a little faster in your next circuit. If it is high, slow down. Don't worry if you do not improve your score each workout. There will be days when you feel less energetic.

4. The Cool-Off

Five to 10 minutes spent cooling off after vigorous activity eases the load on the heart-circulatory system, hastens the recovery process, and more quickly reduces post-effort muscle fatigue and tightness. The more intense the workout, the more need for a warm-down. Without it, it's like a hard landing. During vigorous exercise, heart rate is accelerated, blood pressure increased, and muscles become swollen and tight from the concentration of nutrients in the muscle cells and the accumulation of metabolites (waste products). To simply sit or lie down while the heart rate and blood pressure are high means the heart must do all the work of returning the blood from the extremities back to the heart, and you may feel dizzy or ill. Mild activity of the muscles creates a "milking effect" on the blood vessels; it keeps the blood moving more efficiently on its return to the heart. There is a quicker elimination of waste products and the bloodstream is re-oxygenated faster, hastening the recovery process. A hot sauna, whirlpool or bath, however relaxing, is not a good idea immediately after a strenuous workout. Heat from a sauna elevates heart rate, sometimes to dangerous levels, after five minutes.

Cool-off exercises should be done in a mild and rhythmic manner. The final two exercises are muscle relaxation drills and should not be neglected. Your heart and breathing rates should be near their normal resting levels at the completion of your cool-off. Static-stretch exercises will reduce the possibility of soreness developing in the muscles you have exercised. The number of static-stretch positions is limited only by your physical ability and imagination. Stretch the muscles to their limit for 4 to 7 seconds.

Our recommended program is designed for various pilot ages and fitness levels. Training Table A programs are for those in their 20s; Training Table B for the 30s; and so on, up to Training Table E for the 60s. Each Training Table is subdivided into three levels: Level 1 for those with a lower fitness ranking; Level 2, middle fitness; and Level 3, upper fitness. For example, the correct program for a very fit 25-year-old would be A3; a 50-year-old with a low fitness level would use D1.

Regardless of fitness rating, go through a brief period of preliminary conditioning before starting a Training Table. This gives you a chance to become familiar with how each of the exercises is performed and the effort involved.

For preliminary conditioning, select the Level 1 program on the training table for your age group. Perform the warm-up and optional exercises as listed. In the fitness circuit, however, perform each exercise for the suggested number of repetitions but rest 15 to 30 seconds after each exercise. Do the full circuit twice and don't bother about how long it takes. Do the routine at a slow, comfortable pace, concentrating on the correct performance of each exercise. Then do the cool-off exercises.

This preliminary conditioning procedure should be followed for six workouts. If possible, exercise on six consecutive days. Your first two workouts will be learning sessions in which you make sure you perform each exercise correctly. Your next two workouts will move more quickly. On the fifth and sixth workouts, do the full circuit *three* times, still resting for 15 to 30 seconds after each exercise.

Having completed this preliminary conditioning you will be fully familiar with exactly how each exercise is to be performed and will be ready to begin your program in earnest. Your fitness ranking will determine whether you should remain at Level 1 for some time or move quickly to Level 2 or 3.

If your over-all fitness rating (as shown on your rating chart in the fitness assessment chapter) is in the moderately low, low or very low categories, start with Level 1. Stay on this program until you are ready to progress to the next level. If your fitness rating is in the fair or good categories, start with Level 1 for four workouts then move to Level 2. If your fitness rating is very good or excellent, start with Level 1 for two workouts, move to Level 2 for two more, and then begin Level 3. Better to start too low than too high. It's easy to work up.

If you find the lower level programs challenging, even though your fitness score would tend to direct you to the next higher level, be content to stay at the lower level until you can do it without discomfort.

If you have not completed our home fitness assessment, but have been assessed at a professional testing clinic, ask them to rate your fitness on the same scale from very low to excellent. For each level of exercise program a progression is suggested, beginning with a relatively low number of repetitions and circuits. When you reach the highest workload exercise at that level for at least three weeks (eight to twelve workouts), then move to the next level.

If you can easily handle Level 3 and want to progress further, drop down to the next lower age category and begin at Level 2. When you move to a younger age group, don't divide workout segments into two equal periods. Do the exercises as one continuous 20-minute circuit. Gradually lengthen the time to a 30-minute circuit. If still further improvement is desired, move to Level 3, starting with the 20-minute circuit. Regardless of which program you are following, however, never let your exercise heart rate exceed 80 per cent of the predicted maximum heart rate for your age.

Those working on Training Table A of course, cannot progress to a lower age group program, but may wish to add a few minutes to their circuit time, or set a better personal record for repetitions completed in the prescribed time.

Don't drop more than two age groupings. A 50-year-old pilot in superb condition should not do a 20s program.

After you have selected your starting point, read the instructions for each exercise in your program. These descriptions follow the training tables. List your exercises and record your heart rates and circuit scores on an exercise card which you can take with you when you travel. A sample workout card and a blank card to photocopy for your own use are on the next pages.

In the first column to the right of the routines write in the amount of time or the number of repetitions for that exercise. The circuit score is the total number of circuits and additional exercises completed (in the circuit only). At the top of each column enter two dates. The same workout is usually done twice. The card accommodates thirty exercise sessions. As shown in the sample, you can write in the repetitions you should be adding as you progress. All programs in this section are based on a minimum schedule of three workouts per week. Don't attempt to progress with a less-than-minimum schedule.

The greatest difficulty for most pilots will be to overcome exercise monotony. The same exercises performed the same way, day after day, can lead to boredom and skipped workouts. The continuity will be broken and the fitness program soon terminated. Add variety and a change of pace to your program. Periodically change your program content. For example, do the warm-up, the fitness circuit, and cool-off. Try two optional exercises in one workout and another two in the next. Do the circuit in reverse. Or simply mix up the order of exercises. Whatever variation you try, make sure you don't exceed your total time allowance or training heart rate.

Do a "time trial" after you have worked at one program for two to four weeks. The time trial should involve three complete circuits. Take a regular warm-up then begin using a stop-watch or watch with a second hand. Do the required number of repetitions, going from one exercise to the next as quickly as possible. Keep up the best pace you can manage but rest whenever necessary. Note your time and pulse rate at the end of the third circuit. Then do the cool-off exercises. This, of course, is a complete workout. A periodic time trial is another indicator of your rate of progress. When working against the clock avoid the temptation to sacrifice style for speed. Time trials are not recommended for those in their 60s or with low fitness levels.

Sample Workout Record Card

ROUTINE	3/9	4/9	6/9	8/9	9/9	11/9					
– WARM-UP –											
A. Warm-Up Jog	4 min	4½	5	5½	6						
B. Roll Up and Tuck	15r.	16	17	18	19	20					
C. Seated Spread-Leg Stretch	8r.	10									
D. Back Thigh Stretch	8r.										
E. Willow Stretch	20r.										
– OPTIONALS –											
1. Wide 'n Narrow Push-Ups	3×6/3		3×8/4		3×10/5						
2. Lying Lifter	4 r.										
3. Mod. Bent Knee Sit Back Hold	3×10s		4×10s		5×10s	6×10s					
4. Seated Alternate Knee Pull	6×5s.		8×5s								
5. Arm Curl and Extend	4×3r.										

– FITNESS CIRCUIT –
(Target Heart Rate 135-145)

Exercise		Progression / Values
C1. Stationary "Knee Slap" Run	50	
C2. Single Leg Jackknife	16	
C3. Down 'n Out Drill	10	2×8 min. 2×8½ 2×9 2×9½ 2×10 2×10½
C4. Bent Knee Sit Up-Toe Touch	12	(4 min. rest)
C5. Forward Lunge	12	
C6. Standing Twister	12	
– COOL-OFF –		
a. Cool-Off Jog	4 min.	
b. Torso Twist	20 r.	
c. Pullback and Relax	6r.	
d. Bent Over Sag	5r.	
Pulse Rates After Circuits:	136/144 140/146 136/140 132/142 134/140	
Pulse Rates After Cool-Off:	108 110 104 98 100	
Circuit Scores:	2/4 2/1 2/4 2/0 2/5 2/2 2/5 2/3 3/1 2/4	

PROGRAM CODE:

ROUTINE															
– WARM-UP –															
A.															
B.															
C.															
D.															
E.															
– OPTIONALS –															
1.															
2.															
3.															
4.															
5.															

– FITNESS CIRCUIT –																		
C1.																		
C2.																		
C3.																		
C4.																		
C5.																		
C6.																		
– COOL-OFF –																		
a.																		
b.																		
c.																		
d.																		
Pulse Rates After Circuits:																		
Pulse Rates After Cool-Off:																		
Circuit Scores:																		

106

The following five pages describe the basic pilot fitness training tables designed by the Fitness Institute in Toronto. There is a separate training table for each age group from the 20s through the 60s and, within each table, three levels of intensity.

Beginning Workload
There are two columns of figures for each level. The first shows the beginning workload for each exercise in the program.

Progression Column
The second column shows the workload you should eventually achieve through gradual increases in the time or repetitions of many of the exercises. The transition from the figures in the first column to those in the second should be steady and gradual. Progress at your own pace in easy increments. For example, add 15 or 30 seconds, not a full minute; add one or two repetitions at a time, not five or ten.

Repetitions
The word "reps." used on the charts means repetitions. One repetition is one completed movement in an exercise from the starting position, through the full movement and back to the starting position.

Symbols
The symbol "X2" or "X3" means that the full exercise and number of repetitions shown for the exercise are repeated two or three times.

Rest Period
When repetitions are done in multiple groups, a brief rest follows each completed group. The suggested rest periods, where required, are shown on the training tables in brackets.

Now, turn to the training table for your age group. Check the proper performance of each exercise listed for you, and get started.

TRAINING TABLES

TRAINING TABLE A

ROUTINE	LEVEL ONE	
	BEGINNING WORKLOAD	PROGRESS TO
Warm-up		
A. Warm-Up Jog	3 minutes	4 minutes
B. All Over Stretch	5 reps.	5 reps.
C. Roll Up & Tuck	15 reps.	20 reps.
D. Willow Stretch	10 reps.	10 reps.
E. Bent Over Pull-In	3 reps.	3 reps.
Optionals		
1. Adv. Wide Narrow Push-Ups	6 wide/3 narrow, (rest 60 sec.), × 2	10 wide/5 narrow (rest 60 sec.), ×
2. Lying Lifter	3 reps.	3 reps.
3. Adv. Bent Knee Sit Back Hold	3 reps. of 5 sec. each, (rest 15 sec. after each rep.)	6 reps. of 5 sec. each, (rest 15 sec.)
4. Seated Alt. Knee Pull	4 reps. of 5 sec. each, (change pos'n. after each rep.)	6 reps. of 5 sec. each, (alternate positions)
5. Arm Curl & Extend	3 reps., (reverse hands) 3 reps., × 2	3 reps. (reverse hands), 3 reps ×
Fitness Circuit	**Target Heart Rate: 130-140**	
c1. Stationary "Knee Slap" Run	50	50
c2. Single Leg Jackknife	12	12
c3. Leg Exchange	20	20
c4. Bent Knee Sit Up-Toe Touch	10	10
c5. Down 'n Out Drill	10	10
c6. Standing Twister	12	12

Fitness Circuit beginning workload: Continue this series of exercises for 4 minutes. Rest 2 minutes then repeat for another 4 minutes. Add 30 seconds to each Circuit every few days.

Progress to: Two circuits of 8 minutes each. Rest 2 minutes between Circuits.

Walk about during rest period after each Circuit.

Record Circuit Scores and Pulse Rate

Cool-Off		
a. Cool-Off Jog	3 minutes	3 minutes
b. Torso Twist	20 reps.	20 reps.
c. Pull Back & Relax	6 reps.	6 reps.
d. Bent Over Sag	5 reps.	5 reps.

Record Pulse Rate After Cool-Off

LEVEL TWO		LEVEL THREE	
BEGINNING WORKLOAD	**PROGRESS TO ...**	**BEGINNING WORKLOAD**	**PROGRESS TO ...**
Begin With 4 Workouts at Level 1		**Begin with 2 Workouts at Level 1, then 2 at Level 2**	
4 minutes	6 minutes	6 minutes	6 minutes
8 reps.	10 reps.	10 reps.	10 reps.
20 reps.	25 reps.	25 reps.	25 reps.
20 reps.	24 reps.	24 reps.	24 reps.
5 reps.	8 reps.	8 reps.	8 reps.
5 wide/3 narrow, (rest 60 sec.), × 3	10 wide/5 narrow, (rest 60 sec.), × 2	10 wide/5 narrow (rest 60 sec.), × 3	15 wide /8 narrow (rest 60 sec.), × 3
4 reps.	4 reps.	5 reps.	5 reps.
reps. of 10 sec. each, (rest 30 sec. after each)	6 reps. of 10 sec. each (rest 30 sec. after each)	hold for maximum time, (rest 60 sec.), × 2	hold for maximum (rest 60 sec.) × 2
reps. of 5 sec. each, (change pos'n. after each)	8 reps. of 5 sec. each, (alternate positions)	8 reps. of 5 sec. each, (alt. pos'ns)	8 reps. of 5 sec. each, (alt. pos'n.)
reps., (reverse hands), 3 reps., × 2	3 reps., (reverse hands) 3 reps., × 2	3 reps., (reverse hands), 3 reps., × 3	3 reps. (reverse hands), 3 reps. × 3

Target Heart Rate: 140-150 (LEVEL TWO)
Target Heart Rate: 150-160 (LEVEL THREE)

LEVEL TWO:

0	Continue for 8 minutes. Rest 4 minutes. Repeat Circuit for another 8 minutes. Add 30 seconds to each Circuit every few days.	60	Two Circuits of 15 minutes each. Rest 4 minutes between Circuits.
0		20	
4		24	
5		15	
2		12	
6		16	

Walk about during rest period after each Circuit.
Record Circuit Scores and Pulse Rates

LEVEL THREE:

70	Do one continuous Circuit continuing the exercises for 20 minutes. Add 30 seconds every few days.	70	One Continuous Circuit for 30 minutes.
20		20	
30		30	
20		20	
15		15	
20		20	

Record Circuit Scores and Pulse Rates

LEVEL TWO		LEVEL THREE	
4 minutes	4 minutes	5 minutes	5 minutes
0 reps.	20 reps.	20 reps.	20 reps.
6 reps.	6 reps.	6 reps.	6 reps.
5 reps.	5 reps.	5 reps.	5 reps.

Record Pulse Rate After Cool-Off   **Record Pulse Rate After Cool-Off**

TRAINING TABLE

ROUTINE	LEVEL ONE	
	BEGINNING WORKLOAD	PROGRESS TO .
Warm-Up		
A. Warm-Up Jog	3 minutes	4 minutes
B. Roll Up & Tuck	10 reps.	15 reps.
C. Seated Spread-Leg Stretch	6 reps.	8 reps.
D. Back Thigh Stretch	5 reps.	5 reps.
E. Willow Stretch	10 reps.	10 reps.
Optionals		
1. Wide 'n Narrow Push-Ups	6 wide/3 narrow, (rest 60 sec.), $\times$ 2	10 wide/5 narrow (rest 60 sec.), $\times$
2. Lying Lifter	3 reps.	3 reps.
3. Mod. Bent Knee Sit Back Hold	3 reps. of 5 sec. each, (rest 15 sec. after each rep.)	6 reps. of 5 sec. each, (rest 15 se
4. Seated Alt. Knee Pull	4 reps. of 5 sec. each, (change pos'n. after each rep.)	6 reps. of 5 sec. each, (alternate pos'ns.)
5. Arm Curl & Extend	3 reps. (reverse hands), 3 reps., $\times$ 2	3 reps. (reverse hands), 3 reps.,
Fitness Circuit	**Target Heart Rate: 125-135**	
c1. Stationary "Knee Slap" Run	40 ⎫ Continue this series of exercises for 4 minutes. Rest 2 minutes then repeat for another 4 minutes. Add 30 seconds to each Circuit every few days.	40 ⎫ Two circu of 8 minutes each. Rest 2 minutes between Circuits.
c2. Single Leg Jackknife	10	10
c3. Down 'n Out Drill	8	8
c4. Bent Knee Sit Up - Toe Touch	8	8
c5. Forward Lunge	8	8
c6. Standing Twister	10 ⎭	10 ⎭
	Walk about during rest period after eac Circuit.	
	Record Circuit Scores and Pulse Rate	
Cool-Off		
a. Cool-Off Jog	3 minutes	3 minutes
b. Torso Twist	20 reps.	20 reps.
c. Pullback & Relax	6 reps.	6 reps.
d. Bent Over Sag	5 reps.	5 reps.
	Record Pulse Rate After Cool-Off	

for ages 30 - 39)   111

LEVEL TWO		LEVEL THREE	
BEGINNING WORKLOAD	**PROGRESS TO . . .**	**BEGINNING WORKLOAD**	**PROGRESS TO . . .**
gin with 4 Workouts at Level 1.		Begin with 2 Workouts at Level 1, then 2 at Level 2	
minutes	6 minutes	6 minutes	6 minutes
reps.	20 reps.	20 reps.	25 reps.
reps.	12 reps.	12 reps.	12 reps.
reps.	8 reps.	10 reps.	10 reps.
reps.	20 reps.	24 reps.	24 reps.
ide/3 narrow, (rest 0 sec.), × 3	10 wide/5 narrow, (rest 60 sec.), × 3	10 wide/5 narrow, (rest 60 sec.), × 3	15 wide/8 narrow, (rest 60 sec.), × 3
eps.	4 reps.	5 reps.	5 reps.
eps. of 10 sec. each, rest 30 sec. after ach rep.)	6 reps. of 10 sec. each, (rest 30 sec. after each)	hold for maximum time, (rest 60 sec.), × 2	hold for max. time (rest 60 sec.), × 2
eps. of 5 sec. each, change pos'n. after ach)	8 reps. of 5 sec. each, (alt. pos'ns.)	8 reps. of 5 sec. each, (alternate pos'ns.)	8 reps. of 5 sec. each, (alt. pos'n.)
eps., (reverse hands), reps., × 2	3 reps. (reverse hands), 3 reps. × 2	3 reps., (reverse hands), 3 reps., × 3	3 reps., (reverse hands), 3 reps. × 3

Target Heart Rate: 135-145 | **Target Heart Rate: 145-155**

| | Continue for 8 minutes. Rest 4 minutes. Repeat Circuit for another 8 minutes. Add 30 seconds to each Circuit every few days. | 50 16 10 12 12 12 | Two Circuits of 15 minutes each. Rest 4 minutes between Circuits. walking and breathing deeply. | 60 20 12 15 16 16 | Do one continuous Circuit continuing the exercises for 20 minutes. Add 30 seconds every few days. | 60 20 12 15 16 16 | One continuous Circuit for 30 minutes. |

Walk about during rest period after each Circuit.

Record Circuit Scores and Pulse Rates | **Record Circuit Scores and Pulse Rates**

minutes	4 minutes	5 minutes	5 minutes
reps.	20 reps.	20 reps.	20 reps.
reps.	6 reps.	6 reps.	6 reps.
reps.	5 reps.	5 reps.	5 reps.

Record Pulse Rate After Cool-Off | **Record Pulse Rate After Cool-Off**

	LEVEL ONE	
ROUTINE	**BEGINNING WORKLOAD**	**PROGRESS TO**
Warm-Up		
A. Warm-Up Jog	3 minutes	4 minutes
B. Bent Knee Sit Up - Toe Touch	5 reps., (rest 30 sec.), × 2	8 reps., (rest 30 sec.), × 2
C. Back Thigh Stretch	5 reps.	5 reps.
D. Modified Willow Stretch	10 reps.	10 reps.
Optionals		
1. Floor Push-Ups	5 reps., (rest 30 sec.), × 3	10 reps., (rest 30 × 3
2. Lying Lifter	3 reps.	3 reps.
3. Basic Bent Knee Sit Back Hold	3 reps. of 5 sec. each, (rest 15 sec. after each)	6 reps. of 5 sec. each, (rest 15 after each)
4. Seated Alt. Knee Pull	4 reps. of 5 sec. each, (change pos'n after each)	6 reps. of 5 sec. each), (alternate pos
5. Arm Curl & Extend	3 reps., (reverse hands) 3 reps., × 2	3 reps., (reverse hands), 3 reps × 2
Fitness Circuit	**Target Heart Rate: 115-125**	
c1. Modified "Knee Slap" Run	40 ⎫	40 ⎫
	⎪ Continue this series of	⎪ Two cir of 8
c2. Mod. Single Leg Jackknife	10 ⎪ exercises for 4	10 ⎪ minutes
	⎪ minutes. Rest 2	⎪ each.
c3. Leg Exchange	10 ⎬ minutes then	10 ⎬ Rest 2
	⎪ repeat for	⎪ minutes
c4. Kneeling Push Ups	10 ⎪ another 4	10 ⎪ between
	⎪ minutes. Add 30	⎪ Circuits.
c5. Forward Lunge	8 ⎪ seconds to each	8 ⎪
	⎪ Circuit every	⎪
c6. Roll Up & Tuck	10 ⎭ few days.	10 ⎭
	Walk about during rest period after ea Circuit.	
	Record Circuit Scores and Pulse Rat	
Cool-Off		
a. Cool-Off Jog	3 minutes	3 minutes
b. Torso Twist	20 reps.	20 reps.
c. Pullback & Relax	6 reps.	6 reps.
d. Bent Over Sag	5 reps.	5 reps.
	Record Pulse Rate After Cool-Off	

LEVEL TWO		LEVEL THREE	
BEGINNING WORKLOAD	**PROGRESS TO ...**	**BEGINNING WORKLOAD**	**PROGRESS TO ...**
;in With 4 Workouts at Level 1		Begin with 2 Workouts at Level 1 and 2 at Level 2	
ninutes	6 minutes	6 minutes	6 minutes
eps., (rest 30 sec.), ⟨ 2	10 reps., (rest 30 sec.), × 2	15 reps.	20 reps.
eps.	8 reps.	10 reps.	10 reps.
eps.	20 reps.	24 reps.	24 reps.
eps., (rest 60 sec.), ⟨ 3	20 reps., (rest 60 sec.), × 3	maximum reps., (rest 60 sec.), × 2	max. reps. (rest 60 sec.), × 2
eps	4 reps.	5 reps.	5 reps.
eps. of 10 sec. each, ·est 30 sec. after ach)	6 reps. of 10 sec. each, (rest 30 sec. after each)	hold for max. time, (rest 60 sec.), × 2	hold for max. time (rest 60 sec.), × 2
eps. of 5 sec. each, :hange pos'n. after ach)	8 reps. of 5 sec. each,) (alt. pos'ns.)	8 reps. of 5 sec. each, (alt. pos'ns.)	8 reps. of 5 sec. each, (alt. pos'n.)
eps., (reverse hands), reps., × 2	3 reps., (reverse hands), 3 reps., × 2	3 reps. (reverse hands), 3 reps., × 3	3 reps., (reverse hands) 3 reps, × 3

Target Heart Rate: 125-135 | **Target Heart Rate: 135-145**

	Continue for 8 minutes. Rest 4 minutes. Repeat Circuit for another 8 minutes. Add 30 seconds to each Circuit every few days.	50 / 16 / 16 / 15 / 12 / 15	Two Circuits of 15 minutes each. Rest 4 minutes between circuits.	60 / 20 / 20 / 20 / 20 / 16 / 20	Do one continuous Circuit continuing the exercises for 20 minutes. Add 30 seconds every few days.	60 / 20 / 20 / 20 / 20 / 16 / 20	One continuous Circuit for 30 minutes.

Walk about during rest period after each Circuit.

Record Circuit Scores and Pulse Rates | **Record Circuit Scores and Heart Rates**

ninutes	4 minutes	5 minutes	5 minutes
eps.	20 reps.	20 reps.	20 reps.
eps.	6 reps.	6 reps.	6 reps.
eps.	5 reps.	5 reps.	5 reps.

Record Pulse Rate After Cool-Off | **Record Pulse Rate After Cool-Off**

ROUTINE	LEVEL ONE	
	BEGINNING WORKLOAD	PROGRESS TO
Warm-Up		
A. Warm-Up Jog	3 minutes	4 minutes
B. Lying Abdominal Squeeze	6 reps., (rest 30 sec.), × 2	6 reps., (rest 30 × 2
C. Seated Forward Stretch	5 reps.	5 reps.
D. Modified Willow Stretch	10 reps.	10 reps.
Optionals		
1. Floor Push-Ups	3 reps., (rest 30 sec.), × 3	6 reps., (rest 30 sec.), × 3
2. Lying Lifter	3 reps.	3 reps.
3. Bent Knee Sit Up - Toe Touch	5 reps., (rest 30 sec.), × 3	8 reps., (rest 30 sec.), × 3
4. Elbows Pull Back	5 reps.	5 reps.
5. Palms Up Curl	1 rep., (reverse hands), 1 rep., × 3	1 rep., (reverse hands), 1 rep.
Fitness Circuit	**Target Heart Rate: 110-120**	
c1. Straddle Hop Arm Lift	10 �️ Continue this series of	10 ⎤ Two Cir of 8
c2. Roll Up & Tuck	8 exercises for 4 minutes. Rest 3	8 minutes each. Re
c3. Forward Lunge	8 minutes then repeat for	8 3 minute between
c4. Kneeling Push-Ups	8 another 4 minutes. Add 30	8 Circuits.
c5. Half Squats	10 seconds to each Circuit every	10
c6. Lying Twister	8 ⎦ few days.	8 ⎦
	Walk about during rest period after ea Circuit.	
	Record Circuit Scores and Pulse Rate	
Cool-Off		
a. Cool-Off Jog	3 minutes	3 minutes
b. Torso Twist	20 reps.	20 reps.
c. Pullback & Relax	6 reps.	6 reps.
d. Bent Over Sag	5 reps.	5 reps.
	Record Pulse Rate After Cool-Off	

LEVEL TWO		LEVEL THREE	
BEGINNING WORKLOAD	**PROGRESS TO ...**	**BEGINNING WORKLOAD**	**PROGRESS TO ...**
in with 4 workouts at Level 1.		**Begin with 2 Workouts at Level 1 and 2 at Level 2**	
inutes	5 minutes	5 minutes	5 min.
ps., (rest 30 sec.), 2	8 reps., (rest 30 sec.) $\times$ 2	10 reps. (rest 30 sec.), $\times$ 2	10 reps. (rest 30 sec.), $\times$ 2
ps.	8 reps.	10 reps.	10 reps.
ps.	20 reps.	24 reps.	24 reps.
ps., (rest 45 sec.), 3	12 reps., (rest 45 sec.), $\times$ 3	maximum reps., (rest 60 sec.), $\times$ 2	max. reps. (rest 60 sec.), $\times$ 2
ps.	4 reps.	5 reps.	5 reps.
ps., (rest 30 sec.), 3	12 reps., (rest 30 sec.), $\times$ 3	12 reps., (rest 30 sec.), $\times$ 3	15 reps., (rest 30 sec.), $\times$ 3
ps.	8 reps.	10 reps.	10 reps.
p., (reverse hands), ep., $\times$ 4	1 rep., (reverse hands), 1 rep. $\times$ 4	1 rep. (reverse hands), 1 rep., $\times$ 5	1 rep. (reverse hands), 1 rep. $\times$ 5

Target Heart Rate: 120-130   **Target Heart Rate: 130-140**

	Continue for 8 minutes. Rest 5 minutes. Repeat Circuit for another 8 minutes. Add 30 seconds to each Circuit every few days.	15 12 12 10 15 10	Two Circuits of 12 minutes each. Rest 5 minutes between Circuits.	20 15 16 12 20 12	Do one continuous Circuit continuing the exercises for 16 minutes. Add 30 seconds every few days.	20 15 16 12 20 12	One continuous Circuit for 25 minutes.

'alk about during rest period after each Circuit.
Record Circuit Scores and Pulse Rates   **Record Circuit Scores and Pulse Rates**

inutes	4 minutes	5 minutes	5 min.
ps.	20 reps.	20 reps.	20 reps.
ps.	6 reps.	6 reps.	6 reps.
ps.	5 reps.	5 reps.	5 reps.

Record Pulse Rate After Cool-Off   **Record Pulse Rate After Cool-Off**

116

TRAINING TABLE E

ROUTINE	LEVEL ONE	
	BEGINNING WORKLOAD	PROGRESS TO ..
Warm-Up		
A. Warm-Up Jog	2 minutes	3 minutes
B. Seated Stomach Pull-Ins	8 reps., (Rest 20 sec.), × 2	8 reps., (rest 20 se× 2
C. Lateral Stretch	10 reps.	10 reps.
D. Seated Forward Stretch	5 reps.	5 reps.
Optionals		
1. Kneeling Push-Ups	5 reps., (rest 30 sec.), × 3	10 reps., (rest 30 sec.), × 3
2. Lying Lifter	3 reps.	3 reps.
3. Lying Abdominal Curl	3 reps., (rest 30 sec.), × 3	5 reps., (rest 30 sec.), × 3
4. Elbows Pull Back	5 reps.	5 reps.
5. Palms Up Curl	1 rep., (reverse hands), 1 rep., × 3	1 rep., (reverse hands), 1 rep. ×
Fitness Circuit	**Target Heart Rate: 100-110**	
c1. Quarter squats	10	10
c2. Lying Abdominal Squeeze	6	6
c3. Straddle Hop Arm Lift	10	10
c4. Arm Drill	20	20
c5. High Knee Walk	10	10
c6. Side Bends	10	10

Beginning: Continue this series of exercises for 4 minutes. Rest 3 minutes then repeat for another 4 minutes. Add 30 seconds to each Circuit every few days.

Progress: Two circuits of 8 minutes each. Rest 3 minutes between Circuits.

Walk about during rest period after each Circuit.
Record Circuit Scores and Pulse Rates

Cool-Off		
a. Cool-Off Jog	2 minutes	2 minutes
b. Torso Twist	16 reps.	16 reps.
c. Pullback & Relax	6 reps.	6 reps.
d. Bent Over Sag	5 reps.	5 reps.

Record Pulse Rate After Cool-Off

LEVEL TWO		LEVEL THREE	
BEGINNING WORKLOAD	PROGRESS TO ...	BEGINNING WORKLOAD	PROGRESS TO ...
in with 4 Workouts at Level 1.		Begin with 2 Workouts at Level 1 and 2 at Level 2	
nutes	5 minutes	5 minutes	5 minutes
ps., (rest 20 sec.), 2	12 reps. (rest 20 sec.), × 2	20 reps.	20 reps.
os.	16 reps.	20 reps.	20 reps.
os.	8 reps.	10 reps.	10 reps.
os., (rest 45 sec.), 3	20 reps., (rest 45 sec.), × 3	maximum reps., (rest 60 sec.), × 2	max. reps., (rest 60 sec.), × 2
os.	4 reps.	5 reps.	5 reps.
os., (rest 30 sec.), 3	8 reps., (rest 30 sec.), × 3	12 reps. (rest 30 sec.), × 2	15 reps., (rest 30 sec.), × 2
os.	8 reps.	10 reps.	10 reps.
o., (reverse hands), ep., × 4	1 rep. (reverse hands), 1 rep. × 4	1 rep. (reverse hands), 1 rep., × 5	1 rep. (reverse hands), 1 rep. × 5

Target Heart Rate: 110-120   **Target Heart Rate: 120-130**

| | Continue for 8 minutes. Rest 5 minutes. Repeat Circuit for another 8 minutes. Add 30 seconds to each Circuit every few days. | 15, 8, 12, 24, 61, 16 | Two Circuits of 12 minutes each. Rest 5 minutes between Circuits. | 20, 10, 15, 30, 20, 20 | Do one continuous Circuit continuing the exercises for 16 minutes. Add 30 seconds every few days. | 20, 10, 15, 30, 20, 20 | One continuous Circuit for 25 minutes. |

alk about during rest period after each Circuit.

ecord Circuit Scores and Pulse Rates   **Record Circuit Scores and Pulse Rates**

nutes	3 min.	4 minutes	4 minutes
s.	16 reps.	16 reps.	16 reps.
s.	6 reps.	6 reps.	6 reps.
s.	5 reps.	5 reps.	5 reps.

Record Pulse Rate After Cool-Off   **Record Pulse Rate After Cool-Off**

EXERCISE INSTRUCTIONS

Following are illustrations and brief descriptions of exercises found in the training tables. These exercises are safe and suitable for healthy people who have no handicaps. For those with acute or chronic lower back problems, high blood pressure or other heart circulatory abnormalities, or musculo-skeletal problems such as bursitis or a "trick knee," program modifications are recommended at the end of these exercise descriptions.

WARM-UP EXERCISES

Warm-Up Jog

- *Begin easy jogging on-the-spot or moving about your exercise area. The feet should come off the floor 3 to 6 inches (8 to 16 centimetres) and the hands, arms and shoulders should be relaxed.*

All Over Stretch

- *Assume a push-up position, fingers pointing straight ahead. Keeping your arms straight, allow the pelvis to drop close to the floor while arching the body and moving the head back until you are looking overhead. Hold this position for two or three seconds, then reverse the action, forcing the hips high into the air and bringing the head down, trying to touch the chin to your chest. Hold this position two or three seconds, gently forcing the heels toward the floor, then return to the arch position. Breathe comfortably, in rhythm with the exercise, and perform the movement at a slow pace. One arching followed by one bridging movement is one repetition.*

Willow Stretch

- *This drill stretches the shoulders, lifts the chest, stretches the muscles along the sides of the upper torso, tones the abdominal region and promotes increased flexibility. Stand with your feet about 10 inches (25 centimetres) apart, arms stretched high overhead, fingers interlaced with the backs of both hands facing upward. Bend your upper body far to the right and then left. Maintain a smooth, rhythmic motion from side to side. If you find your range of motion is limited, perservere, stretching a little farther each day. Do not hold your breath. A bend to each side counts as two repetitions.*

Roll Up and Tuck

- *This exercise conditions abdominal muscles and stretches the lower back. Lie on your back on the floor, legs and arms stretched out straight. Swing your arms forward, bringing your body to a sitting position. At the same time, bring your feet close to your buttocks and your knees tucked close to your chest, hands resting lightly on your feet. Return to the starting position and repeat. Count each roll-up as one repetition.*

Bent Over Pull-In

- *This exercise stretches the low back and rear thigh (hamstring) muscles. Stand with your feet together, legs straight at the knees. Bend forward, placing your hands on the backs of your lower legs. With gentle pressure from your arms slowly bring your head close to your knees. Hold the maximum stretch for 2 to 3 seconds, then slowly return to the original standing position. Eventually, try to touch your forehead to your knees. Each forward bend is one repetition.*

Seated Spread-Leg Stretch

- *This drill stretches the back thigh (hamstring) muscles and lower back. Sit on the floor and spread your legs at a 90-degree angle. Keeping legs straight, slowly reach with both hands towards your right foot, bringing your forehead toward your right knee. Hold this position for 1 or 2 seconds then return to the starting position, and repeat the exercise to the opposite foot. A stretch to one foot is counted as one repetition.*

Back Thigh Stretch

- *This exercise stretches the low back and hamstring
  muscles, increasing their elasticity and improving leg
  and low back flexibility. Squat and place both hands on
  the floor about 18 inches (45 centimetres) in front of your
  toes. Keeping the palms flat on the floor, slowly raise
  your hips and try to get both legs as straight as possible.
  Force your heels down to touch the floor. Eventually you
  will be able to get the legs straight without discomfort.
  Do this exercise slowly. When you are able to straighten
  your legs, move your hands toward your feet 3 to 4 inches
  (8 to 10 centimetres). Ultimately you may be able to
  place your palms at your toes.*

124

Bent Knee Sit Up – Toe Touch

- *This exercise tones and strengthens abdominal muscles. With heels 12 inches (30 centimetres) from your hips, and arms stretched beyond your head, swing your arms forward and bring the upper body to a sitting position, chest against upper legs and hands on your feet. Return to the starting position and repeat.*

Modified Willow Stretch

- *This exercise firms the abdominal muscle group and increases torso flexibility. With your feet 10 inches apart, place your hands behind your head, and keep your elbows back. Bend to the right then left as far as comfortable. Looking straight ahead, perform the exercise rhythmically. A bend to one side is one repetition.*

Lying Abdominal Squeeze

- *This exercise tones and strengthens abdominal and hip flexor muscles while stretching low back muscles. With knees bent and palms on the floor, bring your knees close to your chest. Your hips should lift off the floor, rounding the low back. Return to the starting position and repeat.*

Seated Forward Stretch

- *This movement stretches the low back, calf and hamstring muscles. Extend your legs, with hands on knees, and feet together. Reach slowly for your toes, keeping your legs straight and head close to your knees. Hold maximum stretch two or three seconds and return to the starting position. Count one . . . two . . . and repeat the stretch. Never force the stretch or use a fast or jerky action. Stretch only to the point of mild discomfort.*

Seated Stomach Pull-In

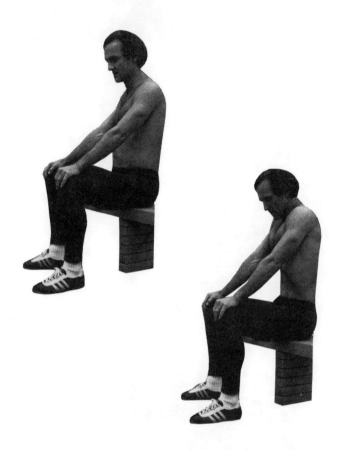

- *This drill strengthens abdominal muscles and stimulates
  the circulation. Sit upright, hands on knees. Exhale,
  drawing in your abdominal muscles as far as you can
  and then immediately relax, inhaling as you let your
  stomach sag outwards. Repeat at a brisk pace. Slight
  hand pressure on your legs during the pull-in action will
  help.*

Lateral Stretch

- *With feet 10 inches apart, slide your right hand down the side of your right leg as far as you can comfortably reach. Repeat on the left side pausing at the maximum reach. Try to reach a little lower with each repetition. One stretch is counted as one repetition.*

OPTIONAL EXERCISES

Advanced Wide 'n Narrow Push-Up

- *This exercise strengthens the chest, shoulders and upper arms. Assume the push-up position, hands 6 to 8 inches (16 to 20 centimetres) outside your shoulders and feet atop a bench or chair. After completing the prescribed number of push-ups (chest to floor), move your hands directly under your chest and do more. Then rest for 60 seconds and repeat. Keep your body straight during this exercise which should be done briskly. Some women may need to do push-ups with their knees on the floor.*

Lying Lifter

● *This exercise tones and strengthens muscles from the neck and upper back to the low back, buttocks, backs of the legs and ankles. Lie on your back, legs straight, arms at your sides, palms down. Keep your head and buttocks on the floor, arch your upper back high off the floor for 10 seconds, then relax for 3 to 5 seconds. Next, keeping your upper back and heels on the floor, lift your buttocks high off the floor and hold for another count of 10. Point your toes away from you and tighten the buttocks. A back lift followed by a buttocks lift counts as one repetition.*

Advanced Bent Knee Sit Back Hold

- *With knees bent, feet anchored, hands on the back of your head, lower your body to the point of greatest stress on your abdominal muscles. Hold for the prescribed number of seconds, return to the starting position, rest and repeat. Some muscle tremor is expected. This is normal. Try not to hold your breath in the sit back position.*

Seated Alternate Knee Pull

- *This exercise strengthens arms, shoulder and upper back muscles. Lift your right foot 6 to 8 inches off the floor and grasp your leg below the knee. With shoulders back, pull hard against your knee. This is an isometric exercise. Your knee doesn't move. Keep your stomach in, chest high, head up, and arms slightly bent. Pull for 5 seconds, rest and repeat with your left knee. Each pull is one repetition.*

Arm Curl and Extend

- *This increases strength in the biceps and triceps. Place one fist on top of the other, your arms extended. Keeping elbows stationary, exert force with your left arm, pull the bottom fist to your chin, with steady resistance from the other fist. Then, without reversing your fists, push firmly back to the starting position. Perform three up-and-down motions then reverse your hands and repeat. You can make this exercise as strenuous as you want. Do not hold your breath. One up and back movement is one repetition.*

Wide 'n Narrow Push-Up

- *A wider hand spacing stresses chest muscles while narrow hand position intensifies the load on the triceps muscles in the arms. See Advanced Wide 'n Narrow Push-Ups for a fuller description. In this version the feet are not elevated but stay on the floor.*

Modified Bent Knee Sit Back Hold

- *See Advanced Bent Knee Sit Back Hold for a description. Note the change in arm position in this modified version.*

Floor Push-Up

- *Note that your feet should be on the same level as your hands, and your arms parallel.*

Basic Bent Knee Sit Back Hold

- *See Advanced Bent Knee Sit Back Hold for a description. Note the change in arm position. Hands rest on but do not grip your knees.*

Bent Knee Sit Up – Knee Touch

- *Begin as a normal sit-up but when your hands reach your knees relax, lower to the starting position, and repeat. Do not anchor your feet.*

Elbows Pull-Back

- *This exercise lifts and stretches the chest and strengthens upper back muscles. With feet comfortably spaced, raise your elbows so your relaxed hands are shoulder high a few inches in front of you. With stomach in and chest high, breathe in, pull elbows far back and hold for 5 seconds. Return to the start, relax 3 to 5 seconds, and repeat.*

Palms Up Curl

- *Place your left hand (palm down) on top of your right (palm up). With arms extended straight down in front, exert upward pressure with your right hand while exerting opposing resistance with your left. When your right elbow is fully bent, relax, return to the starting position, reverse your hands and repeat the action. Each arm curl counts as one repetition.*

Kneeling Push-Up

- This is a milder form of push-up. See previous description of Floor Push-Up for instructions. The one difference in this version is that the knees stay on the floor throughout.

Lying Abdominal Curl

- With hands on your upper legs, raise your head, then shoulders, rounding your upper back and reach to touch your knees. Return to the starting position and repeat.

CIRCUIT EXERCISES

The circuit is a number of different exercises performed one after the other in quick succession with little or no rest during or between the exercises. A complete circuit is usually repeated two or three times in a specified time period.

Stationary Knee Slap Run

- *Run in place, holding your hands (palms down) at waist height. Your knees should slap against your palms. Each slap is one repetition.*

Single Leg Jackknife

- *This exercise involves primarily abdominal and hip flexor muscles. Lie flat on the floor, legs straight, arms stretched out beyond your head. Swing both arms forward and raise the upper body while at the same time raising one straight leg to 45 degrees. Your fingers should brush your toes. Immediately return to the start and repeat with the opposite leg. Perform at a steady pace. Each toe-touch is one repetition. For comfort lie on a thick rug or mat. If unable to touch your toes, touch your ankles and progress to your toes as your flexibility improves.*

Leg Exchange

- *With legs split fore and aft, weight over the front bent leg, arms relaxed at your sides or hands on your waist, quickly reverse the position of your feet and continue at a steady, even pace. Each reversal is one repetition. Avoid up-and-down jumping. Maintain a wide spacing of the feet, and don't hold your breath.*

Bent Knee Sit-Up – Toe Touch

- *This exercise is described in the Warm-Up series but here it is performed at a faster tempo.*

Down 'n Out Drill

- *From a standing position, quickly squat, placing both hands flat on the floor just in front of your feet. With straight arms, immediately kick both feet behind you to a push-up position. Then bring both feet back and stand to a full upright position. This is one repetition. Don't allow your arms to bend when in the push-up position.*

Standing Twister

- *Stand with hands clasped behind your head. Raise one knee high to meet the opposite elbow. Return to the starting position and repeat on the opposite side. Each elbow-knee touch is one repetition.*

Forward Lunge

- *Stand with feet together, hands on hips. Take a long forward step, bending your knee to a right angle. Keep your upper body as upright as possible, weight over your front leg. Immediately push back to the starting position and repeat with other leg. Each step is one repetition.*

Modified Knee Slap Run

- *This is a milder version of the Stationary Knee Slap Run, already described. The difference is the forearms slope downward.*

Modified Single Leg Jackknife

- *This exercise is the same as the Single Leg Jackknife, with the exception that your hands touch the knees, not the toes.*

Kneeling Push-Up

- *This exercise is described in the Optional series. In the Circuit it should be done at a faster pace.*

Roll Up and Tuck

- *This exercise is described in the Warm-Up series, but here it is performed at a faster pace.*

Straddle Hop Arm Lift

- *Stand with feet together, arms at your sides. As you hop to a feet-spread position, raise your arms to shoulder level, then return to the start. Each legs-spread position is one repetition.*

Half Squat

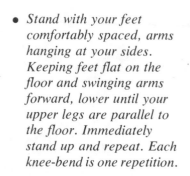

- *Stand with your feet comfortably spaced, arms hanging at your sides. Keeping feet flat on the floor and swinging arms forward, lower until your upper legs are parallel to the floor. Immediately stand up and repeat. Each knee-bend is one repetition.*

Lying Twister

- *This exercise is a lying version of the Standing Twister described earlier in this series. Be sure to raise your head and shoulders off the floor as your knee is brought up toward your chest.*

Quarter Squat

- *This is a mild form of half
  squat, described earlier. In
  this version, your knees are
  bent only to where the top
  line of your thighs forms a
  45-degree angle with the
  floor.*

Lying Abdominal Squeeze

- *The exercise is described in
  the Warm-Up series.*

Arm Drill

- *The arm-pumping action of this exercise tones arm and shoulder muscles. Standing with feet comfortably spaced, quickly bring your right hand up alongside your right ear then swing your arm down as you repeat a similar action with your left arm. Continue at a brisk pace with your fists lightly closed, not clenched. Each arm action counts as one repetition.*

High Knee Walk

- *Walk in place with a brisk, exaggerated high knee action, and an upright upper body. Each step is one repetition.*

Side Bend

- *This is the same as the Lateral Stretch, described in the Warm-Up series but this exercise is performed more quickly with no pause at the full stretch position. Each bend is one repetition.*

COOL-OFF EXERCISES

Cool-Off Jog

- *This should be slow, and relaxed. Keep hands, arms and shoulders loose, more of a bouncing shuffle than a jog. It can be done on-the-spot or moving about the exercise area.*

Torso Twist

- *Stand with feet comfortably spaced, and turn far to your right and then to your left. Let your arms swing loosely. A turn to one side is one repetition.*

Pullback and Relax

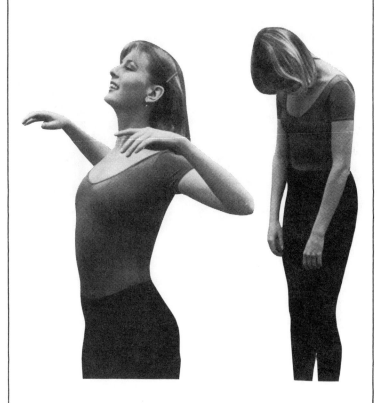

- *Stand with feet comfortably spaced, stomach in, arms bent and raised to shoulder level, hands relaxed. Breathe in and pull your elbows back for 3 to 5 seconds, then exhale in a long, easy sigh and let your arms drop slowly to your sides. Also let your head drop forward and shoulders and knees sag a little. Remain in this relaxed slump position for about 5 seconds, then return to the starting position and repeat.*

Bent Over Sag

- *Stand upright, hands resting lightly against the front of your upper legs. Take a long, deep breath, moderately tightening the muscles throughout your body, then exhale in a long, easy sigh, letting your muscles relax, and your upper body move forward and down, keeping your legs straight. In this position, take another deep breath and exhale, trying to let your upper body drop even lower. Remain in this hang position for a few seconds, then slowly return to the starting position and repeat.*

MODIFICATIONS FOR THE RECOMMENDED PROGRAM

If you have a minor disability or suffer certain chronic aches and pains, some exercises in the recommended program may be undesirable. Following are program modifications for common ailments. You should be cleared by your doctor first.

1. If you have a back problem

Therapy can ease back pain. Surgery is not always needed. Be cautious of accepting the promise of a quick cure. Some back pain can never be totally relieved. Understanding that good posture and exercises will help align your spine, strengthen its support muscles, and·cut down the pain is potent motivation. If your pain is severe, don't try to cure yourself. See a doctor – and don't wait until tomorrow. Back problems are usually progressive. Eighty per cent of all back pain complaints are related to weakness of muscles, tendons and ligaments. Be patient with your exercise program. It will likely take months before you notice improvement. Make these routines a life-long habit and your back pain will probably never again be as bad as it is now. One important habit to develop: take the forward sag out of your lower spine by tightening the muscles in your stomach and buttocks when walking or sitting. It will become habit. Now, on to our modified program.

Start cautiously. If you have more than the usual discomfort or more than "first day" muscle soreness, stop and consult your doctor. Do the pilot recommended program, omitting the following exercises. In their place do the suggested substitute exercises.

Training Table A

Omit All Over Stretch — substitute Seated Forward Stretch (*Training Table D*)

Omit Willow Stretch — substitute Lying Abdominal Squeeze (*Training Table D*)

Omit Bent Over Pull-In	— substitute Back Thigh Stretch *(Training Table B)*
Omit Advanced Wide 'n Narrow Push-Ups	— substitute regular Wide 'n Narrow Push-ups *(Training Table B)*
Omit Lying Lifter	
Omit Advanced Bent Knee Sit Back Hold	— substitute Lying Abdominal Curl *(Training Table E)*
Omit Single Leg Jackknife	— substitute Modified Single Leg Jackknife but do same number of repetitions
Omit Leg Exchange	— substitute Straddle Hop Arm Lift *(Training Table D)*
Omit Down 'n Out Drill	— substitute Half Squats *(Training Table D)*
Omit Standing Twister	— substitute Lying Abdominal Squeeze doing $3/4$ of the number of repetitions shown for the Standing Twister

Do Torso Twist within a comfortable range of rotation
Omit Bent Over Sag

Training Table B

Omit Willow Stretch	— substitute Lying Abdominal Squeeze *(Training Table D)*
Omit Modified Bent Knee Sit Back Hold	— substitute Lying Abdominal Curl *(Training Table E)*
Omit Lying Lifter	
Omit Single Leg Jackknife	— substitute Modified Single Leg Jackknife but do same number of repetitions
Omit Down 'n Out Drill	— substitute Straddle Hop Arm Lift *(Training Table D)*

Omit Forward Lunge	— substitute Lying Abdominal Squeeze but do the same number of repetitions as indicated for the Standing Twister

Do Torso Twist within a comfortable range of rotation
Omit Bent Over Sag

Training Table C

Omit Modified Willow Stretch	— substitute Seated Forward Stretch. *(Training Table D)*
Omit Basic Bent Knee Sit Back Hold	— substitute Lying Abdominal Curl *(Training Table E)*
Omit Lying Lifter	
Omit Leg Exchange	— substitute Straddle Hop Arm Lift *(Training Table D)*
Omit Forward Lunge	— substitute Half Squats *(Training Table D)*

Do Torso Twist within a comfortable range of rotation
Omit Bent Over Sag

Training Table D

Omit Modified Willow Stretch	— substitute Back Thigh Stretch *(Training Table B)*
Omit Lying Lifter	
Omit Forward Lunge	— substitute High Knee Walk *(Training Table E)*
Omit Lying Twister	— substitute Lying Abdominal Squeeze but do number of repetitions shown for Lying Twister

Do Torso Twist within a comfortable range of rotation
Omit Bent Over Sag

Training Table E

| Omit Lateral Stretch | — substitute Lying Abdominal Squeeze *(Training Table D)* |

Omit Lying Lifter

| Omit Side Bends | — substitute Bent Knee Sit-Up — Knee Touch, doing one half the repetitions shown for Side Bends |

Do Torso Twist within a comfortable range of rotation

Omit Bent Over Sag

NOTE: Even with the above program modifications, a particularly sensitive back condition might still become aggravated from activities such as Stationary Jogging, Straddle Hops or some of the sit-up exercises. If you have a back problem, start your program cautiously and increase the effort you exert only as you see that your back is not being unduly affected by the exercises. At the first sign of any back pain or discomfort (other than normal "first day" muscle soreness) discontinue your program and consult your doctor.

2. If you have a heart problem

Few pilots who suffer heart attacks are relicensed. Licensing authorities are behind medicine in recognizing that heart attack victims can be rehabilitated to levels of health not reached in their pre-coronary days. Pilots should be judged on their existing fitness and not medical history. Heart attack victims are often among the most fervent of fitness converts. In his book *Heart Attack? Counter-attack!* Dr. Terence Kavanagh of Toronto describes how his coronary patients have jogged themselves back to health, seven of them completing the gruelling 26-mile Boston Marathon in 1973. Not that the objective of their program was competition, but the fact they competed dramatically illustrates what can be done. More important, it's a psychological boost to each heart attack victim, proof that he is not weak, handicapped, or an incomplete or ineffectual man.

If a man has the health to run 26 miles, 385 yards, surely he has the heart to fly an airplane. Dr. Kavanagh's program should give hope to all pilots who have suffered coronaries and want to fly again, as indeed it has offered to heart attack victims in all walks of life. His methods are based on some assumptions that were taboo only a few years ago. One new assumption is that post-coronary victims are not invalids. Indeed, it may have been the pampering and forced inactivity of previous heart attack victims that contributed to a second and third attack. Under careful monitoring and a progressively tougher workload, Dr. Kavanagh has shown that exercise strengthens the damaged heart.

If you have had or suspect you are going to have a heart attack, it would be foolish to begin an unsupervised exercise program. Get to your doctor. Generally the programs outlined in this book are inappropriate for the immediate post-cardiac.

If the doctor thinks an exercise program would be safe and desirable, he might recommend a locally available facility where a medically supervised exercise stress test and a properly designed activity program could be followed under supervision. If a home-based program is desired, the pilot recommended program for your age group could be shown to your doctor for his comments, amendments and approval. Don't attempt a time trial without his endorsement.

3. If you have high blood pressure

Show your doctor the pilot recommended program and be guided by his recommendations. Don't do isometric, time trials or other exercises which involve straining against a strong resistance. Exercises which include an arms-overhead position, or generally any program which is strenuous and lengthy should be avoided. Never omit the Pullback and Relax cool-off drill and make regular use of the Tension Release program described in the following section on Supplementary Programs. Frequent and mild exercising is often helpful in reducing high blood pressure. Keep comfortably within your capabilities. If you experience uncomfortable symptoms such as headaches or dizzy spells, feelings of weakness or any problem that concerns you, discontinue your program and see your doctor immediately. Specifically, here are the exercise changes that should be made in the various programs:

156

Training Table A

Omit Willow Stretch — substitute Modified Willow
Stretch *(Training Table C)*

Omit Bent Over Pull-In — substitute Seated Forward
Stretch *(Training Table D)*

Omit Advanced Wide 'n — substitute Floor Push-Ups
Narrow Push-Ups *(Training Table C)*

In Level 3, do just 3 × 20 reps. at most.

Omit Lying Lifter

Omit Advanced Bent Knee — substitute Lying Abdominal Curl
Sit Back Hold *(Training Table E)*

Use only moderate effort in Seated Alternate Knee Pull

Omit Down 'n Out Drill — substitute Forward Lunge
(Training Table B)

Omit Bent Over Sag

Training Table B

Omit Willow Stretch — substitute Modified Willow
Stretch *(Training Table C)*

Omit Wide 'n — substitute Floor Push-Ups
Narrow Push-Ups *(Training Table C)*

In Level 3, do just 3 × 20 reps.

Omit Modified Bent — substitute Lying Abdominal Curl
Knee Sit Back Hold *(Training Table E)*

Use only moderate effort in Seated Alternate Knee Pull

Omit Down 'n Out Drill — substitute Leg Exchange but do
same number of repetitions as
shown for Down 'n Out Drill

Omit Bent Over Sag

Training Table C

Omit Basic Bent — substitute Lying Abdominal Curl
Knee Sit Back Hold *(Training Table E)*

Use only moderate effort in Seated Alternate Knee Pull
Omit Bent Over Sag

Training Table D
Omit Bent Over Sag

Training Table E
Omit Bent Over Sag

4. If you have a musculo-skeletal problem

Musculo-skeletal problems can be a back condition, bad shoulder, "trick knee," bursitis of a joint, postural defect, or a weak ankle. There are so many variations it is impossible to suggest specific program modifications to cover every ailment. Using caution, imagination and common sense, chronic musculo-skeletal problems are often helped by following a regular exercise program. Muscles are strengthened, and joints made more flexible. Tolerance to activity is improved.

If you suffer from a condition which you know will react badly to one or more of the exercises in your program then omit that exercise. You can substitute one from another program which works the same area but will be safer. If you are seriously doubtful about even starting your program, be guided by your physician's advice.

9 Supplementary Programs

Don't stop exercising because you're getting older; you grow old when you stop exercising.

1. ON THE ROAD

Despite the interruption of random scheduling and long lay-overs, don't wait until you get home to resume your program. Take your program with you. It is designed so you can do it just about anywhere. If you wish to vary your program or shorten it because of limited time, do your warm-up exercises, omit the optionals, do half of your normal fitness circuit and finish with the cool-off exercises. An even shorter program is your warm-ups followed by cool-off routines. This is an easy way to work off the stiffness and sluggishness of a long flight.

2. A FITNESS WALK

Walking is an effective fitness-building exercise. Start easy and then vary your pace. Walk fast for a block or two, go slow, and then fast again. Try a moderate pace for a while. Walking up hills or stairs will increase the workload. For strength, take two or three steps at a time. Choose new routes. Explore. You are limited only by your imagination and, of course, your fitness level. Check your pulse rate periodically to see that it is high enough to produce cardio-respiratory benefits while staying below your training rate ceiling.

3. A TENSION-RELEASE ROUTINE

Doing the recommended pilot fitness program is an excellent way to keep the stress load of your life under control, but there are some tension-release exercises you may wish to try. They will help your muscles remain loose and relaxed even when you are under pressure. Read the instructions carefully because proper performance is essential to achieving relaxation. Do the exercises slowly.

TENSION-RELEASE EXERCISES

High Stretch and Relax

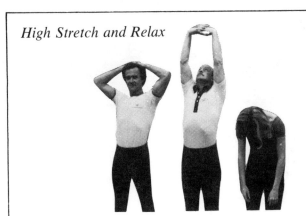

- *Standing erect, place both hands on top of your head, fingers intertwined. Take a deep breath as you stretch both arms high overhead, keeping the backs of your hands facing toward the ceiling. Tilt your head back slightly and lift your chest. Hold this position 3 to 5 seconds, then exhale with a long, easy sigh, allowing your hands to part and drop slowly to your sides. Let your shoulders and head sag forward and the knees bend slightly. During this exhale and relaxation phase "let go" of muscle tension. Imitate a snow man melting in the warm sun. Remain in this relaxed slump position for 3 to 5 seconds then repeat the whole cycle six times.*

Standing Tight and Loose

- *With feet comfortably spaced, hands lightly clenched and resting on your upper chest, bent elbows pointing down, take a deep breath, and moderately tighten your fists and all the muscles throughout your body for 3 to 5 seconds, then exhale in a long, easy sigh. Slowly let your muscles relax, arms drop loosely at your sides, head forward and knees sagging. Slump for 3 to 5 seconds, then repeat routine 6 times.*

Head Circling

- *Stand upright and relaxed. Let your head drop so that your chin is almost touching your chest. Slowly turn your head one way in one complete circle, then the opposite way. Let your jaw sag. Keep hands, arms and shoulders relaxed. Do a total of 10 slow, relaxed rotations (5 each way).*

Rag Doll Jog

- *This can be done on-the-spot or moving about. Stay as loose as possible. Jog slowly, your feet no more than 3 or 4 inches off the floor. Your hands, arms, shoulders, head and neck should be loose and bouncy like a rag doll. Jog 2 to 3 minutes.*

Seated Sag

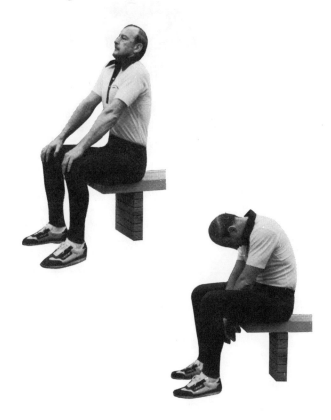

- *Sit upright in a chair, feet comfortably spaced, hands resting on your knees. Take a deep breath and shrug your shoulders toward your ears while moderately tightening the muscles throughout your body. Hold 3 to 5 seconds and then exhale in a long, easy sigh while allowing your muscles to relax. Let your hands slide off your knees between your legs as your shoulders slump and your chin drops onto your chest. Remain in this sag position 3 to 5 seconds. Repeat 6 times.*

Lying Tight and Loose

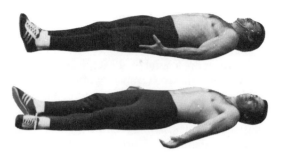

- *Lie on your back, legs straight, arms at your sides and a small pillow under your head. Take a deep breath and with moderate pressure, press your feet against each other and press your hands against your sides for 3 to 5 seconds. Exhale in a long, easy sigh as you relax all muscles. Let your feet just fall to each side and let your hands fall away from your body. Remain in this relaxed position, breathing slowly and deeply, for 10 seconds, then repeat the whole routine 6 times. You might remain in the lying position for a few moments longer to enjoy complete relaxation. You may fall asleep!*

4. YOUR FLIGHT DECK ROUTINE

Pilots, secretaries, switchboard operators and business executives share an occupational hazard: long hours of sitting. The baseball fan's answer is the seventh inning stretch. For employees in business and industry it's a walk to the coffeeshop. Pilots suffer from confinement, but there are a number of exercises you can do while at the controls. Because these exercises will not tax your cardio-respiratory system, they should not be considered a substitute for a training program. Their purpose is to stimulate the circulation and stretch and activate muscles, helping relieve them of the tension and discomfort of a long flight. Obviously only a few of the following exercises can be done by solo pilots without compromising safety.

FLIGHT DECK EXERCISES

Heel and Toe Drill

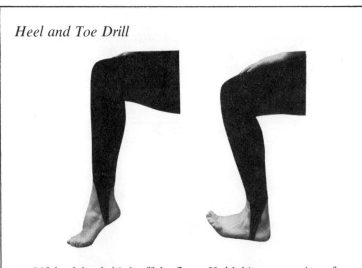

- *Lift both heels high off the floor. Hold this contraction of your calf muscles briefly, then lower your heels and lift the toes high and hold briefly. Continue at a slow pace for 10 heel raises and 10 toe lifts.*

Crossed Ankle Isometric Drill

- *Press the front of one ankle against the back of the other for 3 seconds, then reverse and repeat. Do 10 repetitions.*

Seated Leg Extension and Ankle Flex

- *If you have room, extend both legs parallel to the floor, then point your toes forward and then pull them back toward you. Hold each position briefly for a total of 10 each way.*

Seated Stomach Pull-in

- *Sitting upright, exhale while drawing your stomach in as far as you can. Hold momentarily, then relax, breathing in and letting your stomach out as far as you can. Do 10.*

Arm Drill

- *Start with your arms at your sides, hands lightly clenched. Quickly bring one hand up near your right ear then swing your hand down as the opposite hand comes up. Continue in alternating fashion for a total of 15 with each arm.*

Shoulder Shrug and Relax

- *Sit comfortably upright, both feet flat on the floor, hands resting lightly on your upper legs, elbows bent. Take a deep breath, press down firmly with your hands against your upper legs, straightening your arms and hunching your shoulders high towards your ears. Hold this position for 3 to 5 seconds, then exhale with a long, easy sigh, letting your shoulders drop and your head drop forward loosely onto your chest. Try to "let go" as much as possible. Remain in this position, breathing easily, for several seconds then return to the starting position and repeat. Do six repetitions, each time trying to relax a little more.*

Head Circling

● *This exercise is described in the Tension-Release series.*

Pullback and Relax

● *This exercise is described in the Cool-Off series.*

10 *Alternative Programs*

Run for your life.

World-famous track coach Geoffrey Dyson of Britain says people should not exercise out of a sense of duty. He describes exercises as "physical castor oil," a sacrifice to the new religion of fitness. He warns physical educators against presenting themselves as saviours and advises instead that they should tell people to do physical things that are fun.

While a strict diet of exercises probably serves the body best, it does little for the mind. Our recommended program will not appeal to every pilot. Motivation is so vital to any form of physical activity that we suggest you find activities which are challenging, beneficial, and most important, which you enjoy and will continue doing.

We have been victimized by the media into believing that sports are the domain of super stars. We're so awed by their display of skill, speed and daring that we forget the joy of sports is available to people of all ages and abilities. For most of us sport offers even more to us than to the professionals. Their livelihood depends on it. They are answerable to coaches, management and fans. We can do it for the simple pleasure of doing.

But note that not all physical activity offers equal advantage to your health. Riding horses, for instance, will add little to your physiological well-being, although it is a good way to combat stress. As for cardiovascular benefit, it does far more for the horse. No person or institution has the answer to what exercises or sports are best. Choose one or a combination of sports or activities such as jogging, squash, cycling, rowing, or cross-country skiing, that will exercise your heart and lungs. It is a sad testimonial on our state of fitness that the most popular adult sport in North America is bowling. The only contribution bowling makes to cardiovascular fitness is for the pin setters, and most of these sweaty overworked people have long ago been replaced by machines.

Few of the following alternative activities offer the complete conditioning which has been built into our recommended program. If you choose one or a combination of these alternatives as your avenue to improved physical fitness, augment them with a few exercises from the recommended program. For instance, all activities should be preceded by a warm-up routine such as outlined in our recommended program and if you want to jog, you should do some flexibility, abdominal and upper body exercises before or after you jog.

The following alternatives are introductions, not meant to be full explanations. Most sport and cardiovascular recreation disciplines have their own governing associations which produce manuals and periodicals offering valuable advice. After (or maybe before) you've chosen an alternative, search for the appropriate literature to guide you in the purchase of clothing, equipment and programs. In Canada many of the national governing bodies of these groups are linked with the Federal Government and have offices in Ottawa.

1. WALKING

Advocates of walking can be messianic extolling toe-heel virtues. They talk of its meditative or escape value, how it hones alertness and introspection, how it is available to people of all ages at no cost, and how there is no obligation to follow anyone else's route or pace. For obvious reasons they suggest extreme foot care – powders, massages and daily baths. Intricately conceived, the foot contains twenty-eight bones and three balance points that, along with the other foot, support the whole weight of the body. Walkers may tell you that if you point your toes straight ahead you will save one step for every six taken by a person whose feet are splayed outwardly. They will advise you to get sturdy shoes with plenty of room for your feet. Best are shoes with leather uppers because they let your feet breathe. Walkers may even let you in on a little secret: buy your shoes at the end of the day when your feet are slightly swollen. For a long hike wear a pair of coarse all-wool socks over cotton ones. Now you're ready to explore or meditate. An excellent suggestion for a lay-over! Or even at home. If possible, park your car one or two kilometres from the airport and walk the rest of the way. Gradually increase the distance. Get in the habit of walking up stairs. Elevators were invented for convenience, not health. You may not want to walk up eighty storeys, but get off the elevator four to eight storeys short of your destination and walk up the remaining floors.

Walking's big brother is the recreation of hiking. It has gained in popularity in the past few years because of increased public attention on health and conservation. Proper footwear is the single most important part of hiking equipment because it is the feet that carry the hiker. Keep feet protected and comfortable.

Unless you regularly walk up hills or stairs or carry a load on your back, you probably won't raise your heart rate to a desirable exercise level. And you may become impatient with the long time it takes to reap the benefits of walking.

But, if you're a pilot who has been getting no exercise, walking is an excellent way to start your fitness program. Here's a brief program suggestion:

On the first day walk 10 minutes (5 minutes from your home or hotel and 5 minutes back). Add 1 minute each way every day until you're walking 30 minutes.

After the first two weeks on your program, walk 30 minutes daily – 1 minute at a brisk pace and 1 minute slow and so on. After another two weeks you should be ready for more vigorous exercises such as jogging.

2. JOGGING

A number of books, magazine articles and booklets, both supportive and critical, have been devoted to jogging since it became popular in the early 1960s in North America. Its appeal is obvious. Any able-bodied person can jog. Because it employs the big muscles of the legs it is an excellent cardiovascular builder. It can be done almost anywhere, even in a house, although there are better places. The equipment (a pair of running shoes) and facilities (the great free outdoors) are inexpensive. In the mid-1970s a U.S. panel of fitness experts, commissioned the President's Council on Physical Fitness and Sports, voted jogging the best single form of exercise.

Jogging is a good way to learn about the places you fly to. John Burns, a Toronto *Globe and Mail* correspondent in China, became the first foreigner to run in the annual Around-the-City (Peking) race in 1973. A jogger, not a competitive runner, he prepared by jogging at night around the Forbidden City, his tracksuit inscribed (in Chinese) "Long Live the Friendship between the Peoples of China and Canada." Different from the traditional visitors' sightseeing view of the city, he learned about Peking's all-night bicycle repair shops and restaurants.

As with walking and hiking, the proper footwear is vital for good jogging. Wear light-weight flexible running shoes that allow your feet breathing space. The shoes should have substantial arch supports and 'rolling' heels, instead of flat ones.

To save your shins, the small muscles and bones of the feet and ankles, and the knee and hip joints, find soft surfaces to run on. Grass is better than concrete. Athletes and joggers who train daily on soft surfaces rarely suffer leg injuries. The best jogging trails are packed bark, sawdust and woodchips. If you can't find a grassy golf course or park, wear two pair of socks for extra cushion. Wear light clothes. Plastic loose-fitting outfits are excellent for rain. Bulky clothes that soak up sweat and rain restrict mobility and add unnecessary weight.

In recent years there has been a boom in the sale of sports clothes, particularly track suits. Once the exclusive apparel of dashing athletes, they are now used for mowing lawns and lounging. While clothes don't make the wearer any fitter, good clothes sometimes make us feel better about ourselves and are a reason (if no other ones exist) not to feel embarrassed when running outdoors.

Wash your jogging clothes often. Build-up of soil, particularly in the crotch area, causes chafing. Heavy-thighed joggers may want to apply vaseline to reduce the friction of rubbing thighs. Chafing can get so bad it keeps some joggers at home.

Avoid jogging near busy thoroughfares because of pollution and traffic. Jogging at night, expecially in unfamiliar places, can trip you up. Avoid noonday heat. Ideal jogging is in the cool morning or afternoon one or more hours before or after a meal.

An essential ingredient of jogging is good posture, it gives you a more powerful stride and curbs the possibility of low back pain. Use a wall to take the curve out of your lower spine. Pull your shoulders back and tighten your buttocks and stomach muscles. Walk away from the wall, holding the posture. You may feel like a zombie. Now try to relax but don't relinquish the posture, and start jogging.

Take short economical strides. Try for a heel to toe roll; don't run on your toes like a sprinter. Bend your arms at right angles, swinging them relaxed but firmly, slightly across your body.

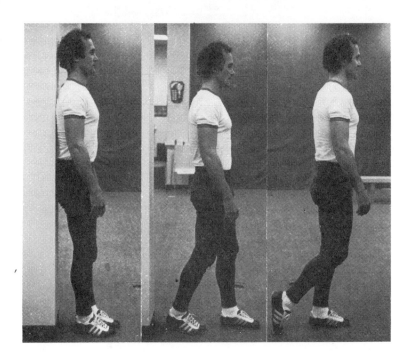

174

Jogging stresses the feet and lower legs, so a special warm-up (different from the recommended pilot program warm-up) is suggested.

A.   *Ankle rotations:* Toes on the floor, heel raised, make 10 clockwise circles with your right foot, then 10 counter-clockwise. Repeat with the other foot.

B.   *Heel raises:* With toes on a 1-inch board and your heels on the floor, raise your body up and down 15 times slowly. This will help prevent pain developing in the achilles tendons, a common problem for middle-aged and older joggers.

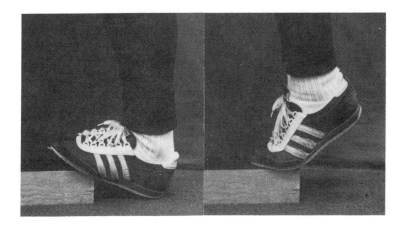

C. *Leans:* Keeping heels on the floor, lean at a slight angle against and facing a wall. Slide your feet out a few inches and hold. Do four positions in total, each for 15 seconds.

D. *Jog-walk-jog:* Jog slowly for 50 metres, then walk for 50 metres. Repeat the jog-walk routine 4 times.

E. *Back Thigh Stretch:* See recommended pilot program section for a description. Do 4 repetitions.

F. . *Push-ups:* For pilots solely on a jogging program, some upper body exercise is advised to reduce fatigue in the arms and shoulders during long jogging sessions. Do 3 sets of 3 to 7 push-ups, working up to 3 sets of 15 to 20.

G. *Sit-up and Toe Touch:* See recommended pilot program for a description. Do 3 sets of 5 to 15 repetitions. Strong abdominal muscles aid jogging and general well-being. Cramps and abdominal weakness sometimes force a jogger to slow down or stop before his cardiovascular system and legs are fatigued.

H. *Seated Spread-Leg Stretch:* See recommended pilot program for a description. Do 10 repetitions.

Now that you're ready to start jogging, train, don't strain. It's better to do too little in the first few days when you may suffer sore muscles and the realization that you may never run a mile in 4 minutes. Maybe not even in 5 or 6 minutes! If you are fatigued, even after a few strides, stop and walk. Aim to reach and maintain a training pulse rate. That means frequent stops to monitor your pulse.

If you run with friends, resist the temptation to compete. You may win! And then lose! The distance and speed you run depends on your fitness and program, not someone else's.

Keeping a diary is key motivation. Record your long-range goals – to lose weight, improve your health, fitness and mile time or have fun – and short-term goals – how much you want to increase your weekly jogging mileage or how many kilograms you want to lose in the next six weeks.

To assist your program, be consistent (jog at least three days a week), plan for variety (jogging can be boring if you run in the same place at the same speed and time every workout), and be patient (don't be discouraged by slow day-to-day progress).

Here are some jogging routines which may help you build variety into your program:

A. In your diary, map out several routes, 1 to 4 miles long. Each jog should start or end at your home or location where you can have a shower and change into dry clothing.

B. Jog from a starting point for 5, 10 or more minutes in one direction and then return along the same route at the same pace.

C. Hill jogging is an excellent way to improve fitness, but it is strenuous. Start up a short, gentle slope and walk or jog slowly down. Repeat 4 to 10 times. Challenge longer, steeper hills as your endurance and strength improve.

D. Fartlek (speed-play) is a kind of 'free-expression' jogging-running. Change your pace often – from a steady jog to mild, short sprint, to a walk or slow jog. Don't follow a pattern of place or pace.

E. Possibly the most effective jogging program is interval training, either on a track or route where short distances are approximately measurable, say, by evenly spaced telephone poles. Taxing both the aerobic and anaerobic reserves, this program has four basic elements: DISTANCE (for example, 400 metres); NUMBER OF TIMES (for example, 4 times 400 metres); PACE (for example, 2 minutes jogging time for 400 metres); and REST (for example, 2 minutes after each 400 metre jog). By adjusting each of these four elements, you can plan workouts to suit your ability and progress.

F. Many joggers advocate long, slow distance. Certainly, burning calories is a function of the distance more than the speed you run. But a time trial every six to twelve weeks will measure your progress. It should be done at sub-maximum effort and only with a doctor's okay.

Following are suggested weekly jogging programs. Do one program for six weeks before switching to another. Choose a workout for your fitness level. After some experience with jogging, you will be able to draft your own program. Notice that these workouts follow a "hard-easy" pattern. Do not schedule hard jogging sessions on consecutive days.

Program 1 (Beginner):

Monday
Warm-up. Jog about 100 metres then walk the same distance. Repeat this sequence four times. Walk 400 metres to cool off. Each Monday add 100 jog – 100 walk to the sequence.

Tuesday
Rest or light 1/2 mile walk.

Wednesday
Warm-up. Jog slowly for 200 metres then walk the same distance. Repeat this sequence twice. Walk 400 metres to cool off. Every second Wednesday add 200 jog – 200 walk to the sequence.

Thursday
Rest or light 1/2 mile walk.

Friday
Warm-up. Jog slowly 400 metres; walk 400 metres; jog slowly 400 metres; walk 400 metres to cool off. On the 4th Friday add another 400 metres jog.

Saturday
Rest or light $1/2$ mile walk.

Sunday
Rest, light walk, hike or alternative exercise.

Program 2 (Average Fitness):

Monday
Warm-up. Jog slowly along one of your routes for $1^1/2$ to 4 miles.
Each Monday take another route of about the same distance.

Tuesday
Light jog (1 to 2 miles or rest).

Wednesday
Warm-up. Jog out and back a total time of 20 to 30 minutes. Each
Wednesday add 2 minutes to your total jog time.

Thursday
Light jog (1 to 2 miles).

Friday
Warm-up. Fartlek along one of your routes $1^1/2$ to 4 miles. Each
Friday change the route.

Saturday
Light jog (1 to 2 miles) or alternative exercise. On 3rd and 6th
Saturdays, do a long, slow distance jog of $2^1/2$ to 6 miles.

Sunday
Rest, walk or hike.

Program 3 (High Fitness Level):

Monday
Warm-up. Jog on one of your routes 3 to 7 miles. Take a different
route every Monday of about the same distance.

Tuesday
Warm-up. Light jog (1 to 3 miles) or alternate exercise.

Wednesday
Warm-up. Hill jogging for 30 minutes. Each Wednesday add 1 more climb.

Thursday
Warm-up. Light fartlek (1 to 2 miles).

Friday
Warm-up. Interval jog. Do 6 to 10 times 400-metre jog on 1st, 3rd, 5th Fridays. Do 9 to 15 times 300-metre jog on the second and fourth Fridays. On the sixth Friday, jog a time trial distance of 1 to 3 miles.

Saturday
Warm-up. Light jog (1 to 3 miles) or alternate exercise.

Sunday
Rest or warm-up. Long, slow distance jog of 4 to 8 miles.

3. CROSS-COUNTRY SKIING

Cross-country skiing is probably the most perfect recreation-sport for fitness building. Because it taxes the arms and legs for long periods of time, it develops all-round body strength and endurance. It is no accident that cross-country skiers are rated the fittest athletes. Cross-country skiing is enjoying a meteoric rise in popularity in Canada and the United States. It is brightening the winter months for people who previously didn't have the money and/or the courage to zoom down hills. It is bringing families together and liberating people who had no place to escape to in the winter gloom. The sport has the advantage of being soft on the bodily joints and the pocketbook. Many of the training principles and programs described in the jogging section can be applied to cross-country skiing. The sport has one danger. It can be so enjoyable that you may not notice you are over-stressing your cardiovascular system. Start slowly on your program and gradually improve your fitness.

4. SQUASH

Growing as quickly as cross-country skiing is squash. Squash courts in Canada are springing up like mushrooms. By the mid-1970s some 60,000 squash players were regulars at Canadian clubs. Squash bags are in view almost as much as brief cases in the business districts of Canadian cities, particularly Toronto where there are probably more squash courts than bars. Once solely a rich man's sport,

squash is now available at reasonable prices at municipal recreation centres, local racquet clubs and YMCAs. Racquets are inexpensive, but expect to break one or more in your first few months of playing. Racquets are lethal weapons so give your opponent swinging room and wear eye and teeth protectors. A lesson or two from a professional will help cure a dangerous swing.

Certainly squash is appealing because of its fitness value. It is a continuous, vigorous, and entertaining activity that challenges people of all ages and skill levels. Like cross-country skiing, it encourages a relatively high training pulse rate while your mind is diverted from the fatigue. Again, competitive exhilaration can be dangerous. Don't overdo it. Take your pulse between games and stop playing before you are forced to stop.

More than fitness, squash is a means of working off steam, a way to release tension after a busy day of flying. The white squash court is not unlike an unpadded cell, a place to vent your primal urges. The racquet is your club, and the ball, the constant enemy. Squash is a chess match, billiards game, social hour, workout, competition, frustration and delight, all wrapped up in a little box. And later you have a shower, a friendly chat with your opponent about your failing drop shot, and then return to civilization.

One criticism of squash and some other skill sports is that the better you become technically, the less you stress your cardio-respiratory system when you play against others who are not improving at your rate. So, in one way it's best to be worst: you will probably be more fatigued than the victor when you come off the court. Challenging people of your skill level is good for your fitness and skill improvement. If for social or other reasons you choose opponents of lesser talent, supplement your squash with other exercises. Aim to play a 40-minute match at least three, maybe four times a week.

5. STATIONARY and OUTDOOR CYCLING

Too often, people will spend hundreds, even thousands, of dollars on a stationary bicycle or treadmill, use it for a short time, and then let it collect dust for years. It is better to invest time and effort in jogging than put money into expensive equipment which won't be used.

But when it *is* used, a good stationary bicycle is an invaluable aid for fitness training. The pedalling resistance can be adjusted and measured. Exacting instruments will tell you the resistance and speed. This means you will know how much work you're doing while you build variety and progression into your program. For instance, you can alternate slow and fast pedalling with light and heavy resistances. Because you're seated, you can easily keep track of your rest and cycling intervals and your pulse rate. With the objective of obtaining a training pulse rate for 15 minutes in a workout, it's simple to draft a variety of programs of 20 to 30 minutes, each having a warm-up, interval rests, and a cool-off. Refer to the explanation of interval jogging earlier in this chapter for ideas on how to plan a workout program on the exercise bike.

A major drawback to stationary cycling is boredom. This can be overcome by watching television as you pedal. It's a novel way to catch the 30-minute national news, a period of hockey or part of a football or basketball game. Keep a mileage diary and record how long it takes you to pedal from the Atlantic to Pacific or around the world. A towel under the bike will prevent perspiration damage to the carpet. The bicycle seat should be high enough so your leg is almost straight and your foot pointing downward when the pedal reaches its lowest point.

As for outdoor cycling, it is one of the very best of aerobic fitness activities. It builds the legs, the heart and the lungs – the threesome that spells cardiovascular fitness. Competitive cyclists develop exceptionally high levels of aerobic capacity, often achieving maximum oxygen uptake readings of 70-80 ml/kg/min.

The outdoor variety offers many advantages. It can be easily adjusted in its intensity, all the way from relaxed coasting to careening at top speed. It's an activity for every age. When compared with walking and jogging, it offers a far greater potential for pleasure. More of the colourful countryside can be enjoyed on a bicycle than would be possible in an equal amount of time spent walking or jogging.

For the best fitness benefits, your cycling program should consist of at least three to five outings each week for a minimum of 15 - 30 minutes each time. Ride fast enough to get your heart rate up to the recommended training level for your age group and be sure to start with an easy warm-up and cool-off with slow, easy cycling to conclude each session. Vary your cycling route from time to time to add interest to your workouts and, as your fitness improves, give vent to the temptation to tackle a few hills.

6. ORIENTEERING

Orienteering is a sport and recreation that combines running in familiar surroundings and navigating with a topographical map and compass. It has the same benefits of fartlek running while enjoying the outdoors. It has the advantage – some might say it's a disadvantage – of not knowing exactly how long and far you will be running. Worrying about whether you are winning or losing, or simply lost, takes your mind off the effort of running. Orienteering was invented in Sweden in 1918; it makes pathfinders out of cross-country runners.

7. VITA PAR COURS

A good general exercise routine is to make a regular circuit of a "Vita par cours." Many have been constructed in parks in North America. These are a series of 15 to 25 exercise stations 50 to 200 metres apart. You follow the instructions posted at each station. Some stations have equipment such as chin-up bars and stumps for step ups. By jogging between stations you improve your total time for the 1 1/2 to 3 kilometre circuit. As your proficiency grows, start on a second circuit.

8. RUNNING-ON-THE-SPOT OR SKIPPING

These exercises are convenient for the pilot who spends much time away from home. They can be done in a hotel room. (One Canadian pilot was running-on-the-spot in a Frankfurt hotel room at 2 a.m. a few years ago when the phone rang. The voice, from another pilot in the room below, said, "Hurry up and catch her so we can all get to sleep.") A good skipping rope – it should be long enough to reach your shoulders while passing under your feet – takes up little room in a suitcase. Skipping is generally a more intensive workout than stationary running, so it won't take quite so long to complete a skipping workout, say 15 minutes. Whatever you choose, stop periodically to check your pulse to make sure it has not exceeded the recommended training rate. Like stationary cycling, these exercises allow you to watch television or listen to music. Run or skip on carpet or wear running shoes to protect your feet, ankles and shins from the hard pounding. Include a warm-up and cool-off session.

9.   WATER EXERCISES

Swimming tones and strengthens most of the major muscles and is an excellent aerobic exercise if it is carried out vigorously. Dr. Kenneth H. Cooper, author of *Aerobics,* says that to develop and sustain an adequately high level of heart-lung fitness through swimming it is necessary to swim about 700 metres in 15 minutes five times per week. In a 25-metre pool, this would be the equivalent of doing 28 lengths at a pace of 32-33 seconds per length. It is possible to start by doing one or two lengths and then rest and repeat several times and increase the number gradually over a few weeks.

Even if you are a non-swimmer, there are a number of exercises you can do in the water to improve your fitness. Because body weight is supported by water, it's an excellent exercise medium for those who are severely out of condition. It can also make some exercises more difficult.

11 Diet and Weight Loss for Pilots

Half of what we eat keeps us alive.
The other half keeps our doctors and
dentists alive.

If we truly become what we eat, then too many of us are becoming
junk. Many regard food only as a means of satisfying the appetite, a
source of gastronomic pleasure, and not a way of obtaining vital
materials to build and sustain a sound, energetic body.

Many aspects of dieting and nutrition remain unknown and controversial, but we do know enough to select the right kinds and
quantities of food.

Native peoples in isolated parts of the world who live mostly on
meat or grain diets and don't eat refined sugar and flour are surprisingly free of civilized diseases such as cancer, hypertension, heart
disease and mental disorders. Dr. Lawrence Lamb, chief of medical
sciences for the U.S. Air Force School of Aerospace Medicine,
noted that people who were deprived of high calorie and saturated
animal fat diets escaped the scourge of heart disease in Europe and
North America after the First World War. During the Second War,
sugar was scarce – a disguised blessing for embattled wartime
people. Over the past century, consumption of sugar has jumped to
an astonishing (and frightening) 125 pounds average per year per
person. Overeating has become a status symbol. Plush restaurants
and television and magazine advertisements make eating a ceremo-
nial occasion. British surgeon Dr. Thomas Cleave suggested that
the correlation of heart disease, peptic ulcers, diabetes and obesity

with geographic location also has something to do with the presence or lack of vegetable fibre (roughage) in diets. Fibrous foods move rapidly through the body and retard the assimilation rate of calories, he said.

We are killing ourselves with artificial, prepared and sugared foods and a lack of natural nutrition. We can blame our own weakness when confronted by the army of food processors who in the name of profit, speed, efficiency and marketing are weaning us from the evolutionary dependence on Mother Nature. At the same time there has never been a period in man's history during which such a vast variety and abundance of nutritious foods have been available. We must search for the natural foods among the glitter of packaged, prepared and instant foods on supermarket shelves. And when we bring home our careful selections we must be careful not to cook the goodness out of them.

Dr. Zak Sabry, head of the federally sponsored Nutrition Canada research group, said that 33 per cent of medical costs in Canada are for the repair of malnutrition. His chief concern is that we eat too much animal fat; the volume has almost doubled over the past seventy-five years.

Other researchers speculate that an irreversible tendency to obesity can occur in children when "nutritional imprinting" – the development of excessive numbers of fat cells – occurs. They say that after the teenage years the body cannot increase its total number of fat cells. Obesity is characterized by the expansion of existing cells, a disadvantage to adults who have accumulated too many in their childhood.

Television does not escape blame for the nutritional decline. Television advertisements promote some of the worst foods and the physical act of eating and drinking, while television itself immobilizes viewers. To get more out of television and life, exercise (and that doesn't mean to run to the refrigerator) during commercials. Avoiding those advertised high calorie (low intelligence) snacks may be all that is needed to reverse caloric imbalance. We are under pressure to buy more fast-order, greasy and non-nutritious foods and eat faster than our forefathers. For many, the family meal is a thing of the past. Now it's a self-serve-and-swift-swallow routine. And when it causes indigestion we further abuse our stomachs with buffering drugs.

Studies on laboratory animals and several surveys of people's eating habits around the world show that the consumption of too many fatty foods increases the incidence of atherosclerosis and senility. A high level of cholesterol, a substance found in eggs, lean and fatty meats, is a risk factor for atherosclerosis, and has reached the "risk" level in no less than 10 per cent of Canadian men. Some researchers are reluctant to link high cholesterol diets with its presence in the blood because the body has the capacity to manufacture its own cholesterol if it is starved of normal food sources of the substance. But this is not to sanction fearless consumption of high cholesterol foods. It's likely that low cholesterol diets are beneficial particularly to people who manifest other coronary disease risk factors.

The volume of sugar consumed by North Americans has risen catastrophically in past decades. It is the major ingredient in a countless number of popular foods, including many popular breakfast cereals. Its abundance is linked to increased cholesterol, obesity, and tooth decay, and does little for health or well-being. Candy rewards and soda pop rank with motherhood and apple pie (which also contains quantities of sugar and unnourishing refined flour) as the North American Way. And to mention soft drinks, the average North American drinks 450 ten-ounce cans of pop each year. We drink considerably less milk. If you crave sugar, seek the natural kinds in raisins, apples, oranges, bananas, figs and pineapple slices, to name only a few foods.

Citizens of the United States consume more than 2.5 billion pounds of coffee each year. Recent studies linking coffee to heart disease and bladder cancer have been refuted by other research. One or two cups will do no harm, but in larger volumes pilots may experience headaches, irritability, nervousness, tremor and irregular heart beats. Dr. Julius Rice, director of the Suffolk County (New York) Addiction and Drug Abuse Control Bureau said that "double or treble (three or four cups taken in quick succession) may cause hallucinatory disturbances and possibly convulsions." It's a seemingly eternal controversy. Until a clear answer is given, the best course is moderation.

While pilots must replace moisture lost when flying at high altitudes, it is suggested they find other sources besides coffee. Humidity is zero at 30,000 feet. Pilots must replace moisture lost in breathing and through their skin. Drinking two glasses of water each hour in flight isn't too much. The water loss of a pilot at 10,000 to 14,000 feet is equal to that of a naked person at sea level on a hot dry day facing a 30-mile per hour wind. The only difference is the pilot doesn't lose as much salt so he isn't given nature's alarm signal, thirst. Dehydration reduces a pilot's performance capacity.

Researchers recently suggested that soft water, deprived of its calcium and magnesium content, is the reason why urban people are more prone to heart disease than those living in areas where hard mineral-rich water is ingested. Theories abound. Pilots must be concerned about the water they drink away from home.

Besides the lengthy list of diseases which accompany malnutrition, one obvious manifestation is obesity. Defined as being 20 per cent or more above ideal body weight, obesity is a disease affecting more than 25 per cent of North American people. Nutrition Canada says that more than 50 per cent of Canadian adults are overweight. The percentage is different for various age groups. Some 40 per cent of the 20 to 39-year-old group is overweight. And 80 per cent of women over 65 are afflicted.

Says Dr. Roy Shephard of Toronto: "The average skinfold has a thickness of no more than 3 to 4 millimetres if the tissues immediately under the skin are free of fat. However, in a typical North American man, the average thickness is increased to 11 to 15 millimetres, while in a woman it ranges from 14 to 22 millimetres, depending upon age; furthermore, readings of 30 or 40 millimetres are not uncommon in the abdominal regions of both sexes. Such massive deposits of fat serve no useful functions unless a twenty-mile swim in icy water is contemplated — they are merely evidence of an over-nourished and unfit population."

In the ideal male figure the chest measures 6 inches more than the relaxed waist. If accumulated waistline fat is visible there will be an equal amount deep within the body crowding the muscles and organs. Being overweight with weak abdominal muscles allows vital organs to sag and protrude and their digestion and elimination functions are hampered. These organs also become vulnerable to injury.

Overweight people usually have a low resistance to food and a high resistance to exercise. The typical overweight person gets heavier with age. His fat expands and his body and heart muscles weaken. Little wonder that obese people die younger — they exhaust themselves! A Cessna 152 engine can't power a commercial airliner; a weak heart can't serve an overly large body. For every kilogram of excess fat, the heart must send blood through an additional 9,000 feet of blood vessels. For the person who is 5 kilograms overweight, this means 45,000 feet! It's ironic that affluence allows North Americans to afford refined and fatty foods that they can ill afford to eat. Many overweight people are hypertensive. Their condition is sometimes relieved by reducing their intake of salt and sodium-rich foods, and generally, by losing weight. Being overweight is also linked to strokes, kidney disease, diabetes, and some digestive disorders. Being fat is a disadvantage to people who require surgery of any kind. Operating on organs under thick layers of fat is a more difficult chore.

Being excessively heavy reduces your chances of living a long life. The Metropolitan Life Insurance Company concluded from a survey of policy-holders that for every inch the waistline exceeds the chest measurement (in men) two years can be deducted from life expectancy. A Russian research project determined that 90 per cent of thin people survive to age 60, but only 60 per cent of fat people are so fortunate. Again, 50 per cent of thin people and only 20 per cent of fat people reach 70, and 30 per cent thin and 10 per cent fat make it to 80. Another insurance company study of 5 million Americans aged 15 to 69 revealed that men who were 10 per cent overweight had a death rate one-fifth greater than average and men 20 per cent overweight had a death rate one-third greater than average.

Obesity is easy to identify and difficult to rectify. So many try, so few succeed. Many say they eat nothing and still gain. That, of course, is impossible. Even magicians can't make something from nothing. Obese people may be unaware that they are snacking. Eating more than three times a day may not be a bad idea as long as they are not big meals. Many animals eat almost all their waking hours. Three meals is an artificial number suited more to the working day than to actual need. Another artificiality is our habit of eating a large dinner at the end of the day. Better to eat a large breakfast, lighter lunch and small dinner so the body has adequate fuel when it is most needed. A Russian dictum is worth remembering: "Have breakfast alone, have lunch with a friend, give supper to your enemy." A person who goes to bed regularly on a full stomach will wake up some day with a big stomach.

Many fat people say they don't know why they gain weight. The answer is usually too apparent: they eat a lot, both at meals and between meals, and they fail to burn off excess calories. Psychologists offer a variety of explanations for overeating. It's a form of self-hate and self-abuse. Or it's a way to find security; food is a friend (who can easily become an enemy). Some people are secret eaters. They refuse to nibble in public and stuff themselves in private. Some will complain they are victims of metabolic or endocrine abnormalities. A recent study of prisoners who volunteered to consume excessive amounts of prepared food revealed that metabolic and endocrine problems were the result, not the cause, of sudden obesity. These problems disappeared when the inmates returned to their normal diet.

One obvious cause of obesity is the failure of people to change their eating habits as they grow older. Between ages 35 and 55 our daily calorie requirement is 10 per cent lower than in our earlier years. And a 55 to 75-year-old body needs 16 per cent fewer calories.

Before you launch into a diet, make certain you need to lose weight. If you have gained weight since turning 25 you are probably overweight. Height-weight charts are an interesting guide but cannot be accurate for every individual. A thin person may have considerable body fat. A heavy person may have big bones and muscles and would suffer unduly from a weight-loss diet. Try the skinfold test, outlined in a previous chapter on assessing pilot fitness, or have a clinic do it for you. A body fat percentage of 20 per cent or more in men and 25 per cent in women means a reducing program is needed.

It is impossible to be selective about the areas of the body — stomach, hips, thighs — from which fat will be removed first when dieting. Generally, fat disappears last from the places it accumulates first. It's a comfort to dieters to know their stored fat is being burned up and that they will eventually have a more pleasing shape and feel better about themselves.

One 37-year-old Air Canada pilot, interviewed for this book, was told by his doctor a few years ago after a routine medical check-up that his cholesterol count was slightly elevated and his tryglycerides were seven times higher than normal. He volunteered for further examinations at St. Michael's Hospital in Toronto where it was predicted he was on a collision course with a heart attack. When he started his special diet he weighed 103 kilograms. Six weeks later, after cutting out sugars and animal fats, and doing daily exercises, he weighed 86. A loss of 17 kilograms. His tryglycerides dropped from a count of 900 to 65 and his cholesterol level fell to safe limits. In the following two years he gained only 2 kilograms.

While his success story is a model of what can be done, it has one disturbing footnote. While learning about nutrition and the undesirable results of self-abusive eating habits, he came to regard prepared foods offered to commercial air line pilots in flight as garbage. "The captains get the lean meat and salad that is offered to first class passengers, and the crew gets greasy chicken," he said. He subsequently decided to take his own food on board. He also discovered that access to good food is difficult on lay overs. Pilots should search for the rare restaurants that provide nourishing, non-fattening foods, he said.

Americans spend $10 billion a year looking for an easier way to lose weight, but there are no short-cuts. Effective dieting is not found in a bottle of pills or an unbalanced diet. Most "10-day diets" are limited because early weight loss is mostly water, and such diets are therefore dangerous when prolonged. And for pilots, crash diets are appropriately named. Fad diets and associated problems, such as dizziness and headaches, are the possible precursors of a real crash.

Convinced that people are what they eat, and ever searching for ways to get an edge on their opponents, some athletes put great store in magic foods — megavitamins, vegetarian formulas, high-carbohydrate cereals and high-protein powders and tablets. Against the time-tested worth of a balanced diet, it's difficult to find wisdom in these excesses. The excess that takes the proverbial cake is the practice by some jockeys who eat regular good meals and then immediately force themselves to vomit so they can qualify on the race scales. They can eat their cake but not digest it.

On the same theme, scientists working for the diet food industry are trying to build indigestibility into certain foods. That means people will be able to eat all they want with no fear of assimilating calories. The research is in two areas: treating foods so they pass through the digestive track without being digested; and developing a chemical which will stop the natural digestion of starches and meat fats. Before the new systems are marketed, producers and governments will have to be certain that people won't starve to death gorging themselves.

Clever quacks remain undetected in the grandiose campaigns to feed our minds with nutritional untruths and our bodies with junk. One of the most damaging campaigns in recent years urged people to give up carbohydrates such as bread and potatoes which provide vital energy for mental and physical functions. Another disservice was the widespread use of pills to suppress appetite or cause a body water loss.

Fasting is supposed to cleanse the spirit, but it is slightly suicidal and causes nausea, bad breath, constipation and a cranky disposition. In fairness to its advocates, fasting is an extreme reaction to a gluttonous society. If a pilot insists on fasting, he should do it under a doctor's supervision. And, all the while, keep his feet on the ground.

When reducing food consumption, it is vital to maintain good nutrition. Skip foods that are high in calories, such as pastries, candies, vegetable and animal fats, fatty meats and alcohol. Buy lean cuts of meat and remove the visible fat. Select fresh rather than preserved fruits and vegetables, and avoid desserts of iced cake and whipping cream. For an energy snack, take a pear and a glass of skim or 2 per cent milk instead of a coffee and doughnut or coke and potato chips. Replace thick or creamy soups with consommé. High in nutritional value are oatmeal cookies, bran or cornmeal muffins, whole grain breads, shredded wheat and oatmeal cereals. Use of a polyunsaturated fat such as corn oil is a good substitute for high-cholesterol saturated fats. Many desserts and sweets are high in calories and cholesterol. Similarly, meat, poultry (particularly egg yolks) and dairy products are high in cholesterol and saturated fats, but have many redeeming nutritional qualities.

A vegetarian diet is an easy way to avoid saturated fats. Vegetarians enjoy a lower incidence of heart disease and are not subject to some types of cancer. But before you stock up on non-flesh foods make certain your diet contains a proper variety and volume of proteins including the essential amino acids. An ill-planned vegetarian diet can be a health disaster; a good one has much to recommend it. It's a way to cut down on protein and fats which are too abundant in the North American meat-oriented diet. Daily nutrient balance should be approximately 15 per cent protein, 25 per cent fat, and 60 per cent carbohydrate. (Fat intake by many North Americans is more than 40 per cent of their total calories.)

Health and Welfare Canada recommends that the following foods should be included in a daily diet:

$1^1/_2$ to 4 cups of milk
2 servings of fruit or juice
1 serving of potatoes (or 2 ounces of other vegetables)
1 serving of whole grain cereal, and bread (with butter or fortified margarine)
1 serving of meat, fish, poultry or a meat alternate (peanut butter, dried beans and peas), and eggs and cheese at least 3 times per week.

Following is a table of foods and their cholesterol content (milligrams) for a 100-gram portion:

Beef, raw	70	Ice cream	45
Butter	250	Kidney, raw	375
Cheddar cheese	100	Lamb, raw	70
Creamed cottage cheese	15	Liver, raw	300
Cheese spread	65	Lobster meat	200
Chicken, raw	60	Margarine, vegetable fat	0
Crab	125	Milk, whole	11
Egg, whole	550	Milk, skim	3
Egg white	0	Oysters	200
Egg yolk, fresh	1,500	Pork	70
Fish fillet	70	Shrimp	125
Heart, raw	150	Veal	90

Sometimes sensible dieting is possible only when the overweight person undergoes a fundamental and permanent change of attitude. Dieting is not starving but it does take resolve to say no to some foods. Keeping a dietary log helps. Who can lie to his diary? Self-promised rewards, say a night out or a new squash racquet (not food!), are good motivators. Avoid situations where food in delicious abundance is being served. Instead of ordering pizza, chicken or french fries, go for a walk or jog. Think about the bad results, not the taste, of eating the wrong foods. Allow a short time to eat and don't gulp it down. Don't eat and watch television or read the paper at the same time or you could end up eating too much. Try starting each meal with a glass of water or juice, or a bowl of consommé. This may remove the edge from your appetite. Smaller plates will make your portions seem larger. Don't skip a meal, or you will be tempted to eat more than twice as much in the next one. If you sometimes do the family shopping, do it on a full stomach. Resist junk foods in fancy packages.

Don't think of your new eating habits as a temporary, dietary interlude; it's a program for the rest of your life.

Start each day with a nutritious breakfast. A recent poll showed that almost 50 per cent of Americans fail to have a useful breakfast. A missed breakfast is too often followed by a listless morning and an overly large lunch. Pilots should not fly if they haven't eaten within the preceding five hours. Without breakfast, pilots can be irascible with passengers and air traffic controllers, and their responses to danger can be slower and inappropriate. Efficiency and self-esteem are heightened for the full day after a balanced breakfast of protein and a measure of fats and carbohydrates. The fats and protein retard the absorption of sugar into the bloodstream so that higher energy levels are maintained throughout the morning. A breakfast of coffee, toast and jam offers only a few moments of adequate blood sugar.

Pilots taking in less than 1,800 calories a day may require vitamin and mineral supplements, although the controversy over vitamins is unresolved. Experts say that vitamins taken in large quantities are unnecessary or essential, impotent or dangerous. Extravagant claims have been made for vitamin E: that it will grow hair on bald heads, reduce arthritic pain, clear up skin blemishes, thin out blood cholesterol, improve energy and sexual appetites, and eliminate under-arm odours. Equally sensational are the miracle attributes assigned to vitamin C: that it can prevent the common cold and reduce blood cholesterol. Vitamin C is depleted by endurance exercises, so a small daily supplement is advised for those on a regular fitness program. But mega-vitamin C treatment may destroy vitamin B 12 and cause the formation of kidney stones. Some people take a multiple vitamin supplement. They believe that it doesn't

196

hurt, but it may not help.

The formula for losing weight is simple — burn more calories than you consume. Make the difference between intake and output only a slight number of calories. It will not bring about immediately dramatic results, but the cumulative effect over several months or a year will be rewarding. Losing 200 to 300 calories a day is about 1 kilogram a month, 12 in one year and 24 in two. Rapid decreases often cause fatigue, headaches and other illnesses and are invariably followed by rapid weight gains. Drastic weight losses can make people irritable, discouraged, and most of all, hungry.

To determine the approximate number of calories (including those required for basic metabolism) you should have each day to maintain you existing weight: multiply your normal or desired bodyweight by

15 (if you lead a sedentary life)
18 (if you are only moderately active)
20 (if you are quite active)
23 (if you do moderately heavy manual work or exercise each day)
27 (if you do heavy work or exercise daily)

For instance, if your desired weight is 175 pounds (80 kilograms), and you are moderately active, then you will need (175 × 18) 3,150 calories daily. To lose weight, don't exceed a number slightly lower, say 2,850 or 2,950. (One pound is equivalent to 3,500 calories).

CALORIC CONTENT OF COMMON FOODS

Food	Measure	Calories
Beverages:		
Milk, whole (3.5% fat)	1 cup	160
Milk, skim	1 cup	90
Milk, partially skimmed (2%)	1 cup	123
Buttermilk (from skim milk)	1 cup	90
Cocoa (with whole milk)	1 cup	245
Tonic Water or Ginger Ale	12 oz	115
Cola	12 oz	145
Beer	12 oz	150
Gin, rum, vodka, whiskey	1½ oz	105
Wine, table	3½ oz	85
Tea or coffee (black, no sugar)	—	0

Fats and Oils:

Butter or Margarine	1 tbsp	100
Butter	1 pat	35
Mayonnaise	1 tbsp	100
Salad Dressing, French (regular)	1 tbsp	59
Salad Dressing, French (low cal.)	1 tbsp	13
Salad Dressing, Thousand Island	1 tbsp	50
Salad Dressing, Blue Cheese	1 tbsp	75

Yoghurt, Eggs and Cheese

Yoghurt, plain (partially skimmed milk)	6 oz	112
Yoghurt, fruit flavoured (partially skimmed milk)	6 oz	170
Camembert	1 oz	84
Cheddar (1″ cube)	1 oz	116
Cottage cheese, creamed	1 cup	240
Cottage cheese, not creamed	1 cup	170
Swiss cheese, natural	1 oz	105
Swiss cheese, processed, gruyere	1 oz	115
Eggs, large, raw or cooked	1 egg	80
Eggs, scrambled, with milk and fat	1 egg	110
Eggs, fried	1 egg	113

Meat, Poultry, Fish:

Ground beef, broiled	3 oz	245
Steak, broiled, relatively fat	3 oz	330
Steak, broiled, lean only	2 oz	115
Stewing beef or pot roast, lean and fat	3 oz	220
Corned beef	3 oz	185
Bacon, back, sliced	1 slice	65
Bacon, side, fried crisp	2 slices	90
Ham, lean and fat, roasted	3 oz	245
Ham, boiled, sliced	2 oz	135
Pork chop, lean and fat	2.3 oz	260
Spareribs, 1³/₄″ pieces	6 pieces	123
Liver, beef, fried	2 oz	130
Liver, chicken, fried	2 livers	148
Chicken, breast, cooked, flesh and skin only	2.7 oz	155
Chicken, drumstick, fried	2.1 oz	90
Turkey, roast, meat only	3 oz	160
Luncheon meats	2 oz	165
Halibut, grilled with butter	3 oz	146
Herring, grilled	1 herring	217
Lobster, boiled & 2T butter	1 lobster	308
Mackerel, cooked	3 oz	200
Ocean perch, breaded, fried	3 oz	195
Oysters, raw, meat only	1 cup	160
Salmon, fresh, fried in butter	3 oz	155
Shrimp, raw, 20 small	²/₃ cup	91
Shrimp, fried 1 large 15 g.	6 approx.	225
Sole, fillet, in butter	3 oz	172
Trout, raw	3¹/₂ oz	167
Tuna, canned, solids only	3 oz	170

Food	Measure	Calories

Vegetables:

Food	Measure	Calories
Asparagus, green, cooked, drained	4 spears	10
Beans, Lima, cooked, drained	1 cup	190
Beans, Green or Yellow cooked	1 cup	30
Beets, cooked, diced or sliced	1 cup	55
Broccoli, cooked, drained	1 cup	40
Brussels Sprouts, cooked	1 cup	55
Cabbage, cooked, finely shredded	1 cup	35
Carrots, raw, whole	1 carrot	20
Carrots, cooked, diced	1 cup	45
Cauliflower, cooked	1 cup	25
Celery, raw	1 stalk	5
Corn, sweet cooked	1 ear	70
Corn, sweet, canned, kernels	1 cup	140
Corn, sweet, canned, cream style	1 cup	187
Lettuce, raw, iceberg	1 head	60
Lettuce, raw, leaves	2 large	10
Mushrooms, fresh, sauteed	4 av'g	78
Onions, raw	1 onion	40
Onions, fried	1/2 cup	176
Peas, green, cooked	1 cup	115
Potatoes, baked, peeled after baking	1 potato	90
Potatoes, french fried, cooked in deep fat	10 pieces	155
Potatoes, mashed, milk & butter added	1 cup	185
Potato chips	10 chips	115
Spinach, cooked	1 cup	40
Squash, cooked, summer, diced	1 cup	30
Squash, cooked, winter, mashed	1 cup	130
Tomatoes, raw	1 tomato	35
Tomato juice, canned	1 cup	45
Turnips, cooked, cubes	1/2 cup	35

Fruits, Fruit Juices:

Food	Measure	Calories
Apples raw	1 apple	70
Apple Juice, canned	1 cup	120
Apple Sauce, canned, sweetened	1 cup	230
Avocados, whole fruit, raw	1 avocado	370
Bananas, raw	1 banana	100
Cantaloupe, raw medium	1/2 melon	60
Grapefruit, raw, medium	1/2 g'fruit	45
Grapefruit juice, canned, sweetened	1 cup	130
Grapes, raw, Canadian type	30 grapes	106
Oranges, raw	1 orange	65
Orange juice, fresh	1 cup	110
Peaches, raw, medium	1 peach	35
Peaches, canned, in syrup	1 cup	200
Pears, raw	1 pear	100
Pears, canned, in syrup	1 cup	195
Raisins, seedless	1 cup	480
Raspberries, raw	1 cup	70
Strawberries, raw	1 cup	55
Strawberries, frozen, 10 oz carton	1 carton	310
Watermelon, raw	1 wedge	115
Fruit Flavoured Breakfast drinks, canned	1 cup	135

Breads, cereals:

White, enriched	1 slice	82
Whole wheat, 60%	1 slice	72
Rye, dark	1 slice	79
Cornflakes, plain	1 cup	80
Cornflakes, sugar coated	1 cup	107
Oatmeal or rolled oats, cooked	1 cup	130
Wheat, shredded	1 biscuit	80
Wheat, flakes	1 cup	105

Sugars, Desserts, Candies:

White cake, 2 layer, chocolate icing	1 piece	250
Fruitcake, dark	1 slice	55
Oatmeal cookie,	1 biscuit	86
Danish pastry	1 pastry	275
Doughnuts, cake type	1	125
Eclair, chocolate, custard filing	1	315
Pie, apple, cherry or blueberry	1 piece	400
Pie, pumpkin	1 piece	320
Caramels, plain or chocolate	1 oz	115
Chocolate, milk, plain	1 oz	145
Hard candy	1 oz	110
Ice cream, regular,	1 cup	255
Sugar, white, granulated	1 tbsp.	40
Sugar, brown	1 tbsp.	43
Honey, strained	1 tbsp.	65
Jams	1 tbsp.	55
Syrup, maple	1 tbsp.	50

Snacks:

Popcorn, with oil and salt	1 cup	40
Popcorn, sugar coated	1 cup	135
Pizza, cheese	1 5½" sector	185
Pizza, sausage	1 5½" sector	315
Peanuts, roasted, salted, halves	1 cup	840
Cashew nuts, roasted	1 cup	785
Potato chips	10 chips	115

Most people don't get fat eating too much; they exercise too little. Even their minimum intake of calories isn't being used. Human bodies are designed to take in more food and do more exercise than most of us do. To avoid obesity most of us will have to exercise more or feel hungry for the rest of our lives. Of course, there's one exercise that is more effective than all others. It's called the "push-away." Push away from the table before taking the second helping.

Exercise moderates the appetite and performs the better-known service of using calories. An excessive appetite doesn't naturally occur after a day of heavy physical labour. It is sedentary people, more than others, who usually eat more than they need. Critics of using exercise as a dietary aid say a person must walk a mile to lose a fraction of a pound. What they neglect to say is that the person is losing weight, replacing burdensome fat with lean muscle tissue, giving the body a more aesthetically pleasing shape and improving all-round body tone and health. On a diet without exercising a person will lose lean as well as fat tissues. A diet and exercise regimen uses stored fats and preserves lean tissue. For the mildly overweight, exercises alone may reverse the caloric balance so that no cutback in eating is necessary. Unfortunately, much advice about weight loss comes from doctors who are taught more about medication than exercise and have a justifiable fear that obese patients are poor risks on exercise programs. And few of the popular books on dieting give more than a passing glance at the value of exercise in weight control.

Obesity makes it more difficult to exercise, and a lack of exercise contributes to obesity. It takes time and courage to get off that merry-go-round. On a sensible diet-and-exercise program some people become disappointed because they are not losing weight fast enough, especially aroung the mid-section where weight seems to be added or lost at a greater rate. Doing exercises in water (buoyancy opposes the force of gravity) is often helpful for an overweight person launching his fitness program.

Normally active people consume calories directly proportional to their calorie expenditure, but this is not the case for those at each end of the activity scale. Inactive people often consume more, and extremely active people fewer, calories than they need. The following chart, based on a study of laboratory rats by the renowned nutritionist, Dr. Jean Mayer of the United States, illustrates how calorie intake changes with the level of activity.

While the immediate effect of exercising is to curb the appetite, you will be hungry after a rest of one or more hours. Don't fight the hunger in the first weeks of your diet-and-exercise program; it is difficult enough doing the exercises without the added burden of a haunting hunger. If you're burning a lot of calories, keep putting logs on the fire! Later, when you're more comfortable with exercising, begin subtle reductions in your eating. To curb your appetite, try exercising shortly before your dinner. You will feel hungry later but will be away from the table where it's easier to resist satisfying your hunger.

You may discover there is no weight loss in the first few days.

Even if there is, it may be from water loss. A long workout can cause a body weight loss of $1^{1}/_{2}$ to 3 kilograms. But this is superficial and will be regained quickly when you quench your thirst. So it is better to measure the effectiveness of your reducing program from week to week, not day to day. Besides recording your weight loss in a diary, periodically measure your waist, hips and upper thighs to keep track of the shrinkage.

Considerable reserves of energy are needed for exercises; that means that diets must be bolstered with muscle-building proteins

Relationship of Voluntary Calorie Intake to Activity Level

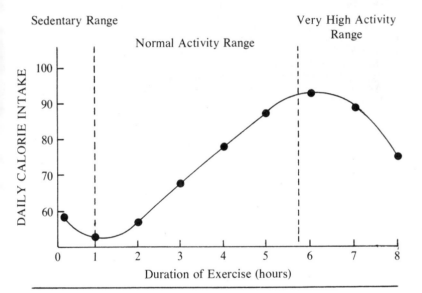

and energizing carbohydrates. Experiments on Swedish athletes by Dr. Per-Olof Astrand showed that high-carbohydrate diets build up stores of glycogen in the muscles and prolong the potential work period. The "carbohydrate overload" system adopted by long distance runners, cyclists, cross-country skiers, and swimmers extends as much as threefold the maximum work time of that provided by a strict fat and protein diet. To gain adequate benefits from carbohydrate overload the athlete first starves himself of carbohydrates for a few days, which makes the body greedy to store an

202

Energy required by a 154-pound (70-kilogram) man for various physical activities*

Activity	Total Calories per hour	Activity	Total Calories per hour
Sleeping	70	Swimming sidestroke, 1 m.p.h.	550
Lying quietly	80	Weight training	
Sitting	100	(moderate weights)	500
Mental work seated	105	Walking up 8.6% grade, 3.5 m.p.h.	560
Standing	110	Figure skating	570
Driving a car	140	Walking up 10% grade, 3.5 m.p.h.	580
Office work	145	Walking up stairs, 2 m.p.h.	590
Housekeeping	150	Skiing, downhill, using tow	600
Calisthenics	160	Squash	600
Walking, 2 m.p.h.	170	Mountain climbing	600
Walking up stairs, 1 m.p.h.	180	Fencing	630
Horseback riding, slow	180	Skating 11 m.p.h.	640
Riding a bicycle, 5.5 m.p.h.	190	Rowing, 3.5 m.p.h.	660
Walking down stairs, 2 m.p.h.	200	Snowshovelling, medium snow,	
Bricklaying	205	10 shovels/min.	660
House painting	210	Horizontal running, 5.7 m.p.h.	720
Dancing, moderate	250	Skiing, cross-country	720
Curling	250	Walking up 14.4% grade,	
Swedish gymnastics	260	3.5 m.p.h.	740
Baseball (except pitcher)	280	Walking in 12-18 in. snow	760
Horizontal walking, 3.5 m.p.h.	290	Skating, 13 m.p.h.	780
Rowing for pleasure	300	Wrestling	790
Dancing, vigorous	340	Tennis (singles)	800
Table tennis	345	Horizontal running, 7 m.p.h.	870
Horizontal walking, 3 m.p.h.,		Marathon running	990
carrying 43 lb. load	350	Football	1,000
Walking up 3% grade, 3.5 m.p.h.	370	Horizontal running, 11.4 m.p.h.	1,300
Golf, with caddie	375	Rowing, 12 m.p.h.	1,500
Baseball pitcher	390	Swimming crawl stroke,	
Pick and shovel work	400	2.2 m.p.h.	1,600
Swimming breaststroke, 1 m.p.h.	410	Swimming breaststroke,	
Bicycle riding, rapid	415	2.2 m.p.h.	1,850
Golf, pulling cart	420	Swimming backstroke,	
Swimming crawl stroke,		2.2 m.p.h.	2,000
1 m.p.h.	420	Horizontal running, 13.2 m.p.h.	2,330
Tennis, doubles	425	Horizontal running, 14.8 m.p.h.	2,880
Chopping wood	450	Swimming sidestroke,	
Skating, 9 m.p.h.	470	2.2 m.p.h.	3,000
Swimming backstroke, 1 m.p.h.	500	Horizontal running, 18.9 m.p.h.	9,480

inordinate quantity. This method is not recommended for pilots doing regular exercises because excesses in this diet can be physically harmful.

Initial consideration of calorie expenditure charts can be discouraging. An average-sized person has to walk 30 or more miles to lose half a kilogram of body fat. Jogging and dancing calorie losses aren't much faster. But the benefits of this program, although long range, are outstanding. Note that the locomotion activities, in which large muscles propel the body over distances (or the equivalent on a treadmill or stationary bicycle), generally use more calories. After exercise, the body continues to burn calories — called afterburn — for up to six hours at a higher-than-resting rate.

*The oxygen consumptions from which the caloric values in this table have been calculated are only approximations. Variables that must be considered in any interpretation of this table are size, body type and age of the subjects, differences between individuals of the same build, physical fitness and skill in the particular activity, nutritional condition, and environmental conditions (whether they help or hinder the individual).
From: *Physiology of Exercise* by Laurence E. Morehouse, Ph.D., and Augustus T. Miller, Jr., M.D., Ph.D., C.V. Mosby 1971.